KT-475-194

A STORY THAT HAPPENS

Dan O'Brien is an internationally produced and published playwright and poet whose recognition includes a Guggenheim Fellowship in Drama, the Horton Foote Prize, the Edward M. Kennedy Prize, two PEN America Awards, and a shortlisting for an Evening Standard Drama Award. His three poetry collections published in the UK by CBe are *War Reporter* (Fenton Aldeburgh Prize; Forward shortlisted), *New Life*, and *Scarsdale*. He lives in Los Angeles.

also by Dan O'Brien

PLAYS

The House in Scarsdale: A Memoir for the Stage

The Body of an American

Dan O'Brien: Plays One (The Body of an American,
The House in Hydesville, The Cherry Sisters Revisited,
The Voyage of the Carcass, The Dear Boy)

The Angel in the Trees and Other Monologues

Key West

'Will You Please Shut Up?'

either/or

An Irish Play

The Last Supper Restoration

POETRY

New Life

Scarsdale

War Reporter

DAN O'BRIEN

A Story that Happens

On Playwriting, Childhood, & Other Traumas

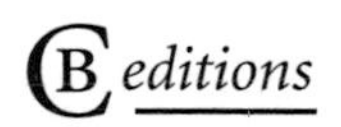

First published in 2021
by CB editions
146 Percy Road London W12 9QL
www.cbeditions.com

Printed in England by Blissetts, London W3 8DH

ISBN 978–1–909585–38–6

For Bebe,
our reason for being

November 1

Time and the Theatre / 2017 7

Unspeakable: Speech Onstage / 2018 29

Surviving Conflict / 2019 49

Identity in Crisis / 2020 72

Acknowledgments 98

November

I wrote these essays during the Trump years, one every summer as craft lectures that I then delivered at the Sewanee Writers' Conference, an annual gathering of playwrights, poets, and fiction writers at the University of the South in Tennessee. I shared this collection's final essay, 'Identity in Crisis', with a master class of conference playwrights via Zoom due to the pandemic. 'Surviving Conflict' received a second airing in September 2019 at the US Air Force Academy in Colorado Springs before an audience of about a thousand cadets in their dress blues, chaperoned by the English & Fine Arts faculty, assorted department heads, the Dean (a Brigadier General), and a handful of retired generals. Some stood to applaud when I finished. Everybody was polite. Afterward two cadets spoke with me—allusively, guardedly—about sexual assaults on campus; another about his abusive father. Many cadets told their instructors, and their instructors told me, that they had been confused by my criticism of 'our President', and offended when I referred to lethal military action as 'state-sanctioned murder' (see p. 64).

I was halfway out the door, feeling as if I were about to get away with something, when a disarmingly cherubic cadet asked if he might pray for me. I said, 'Sure.' He proceeded to pray for me right then and there, out loud, eyes closed, palms up, his lightly freckled face lifted toward the Exit sign, though I can't for the life of me remember what words he used.

It's my hope that these four essays might convey a minor chronicle of these last four dramatic and traumatic years; four years in which both my wife and I have outlived our cancer treatments, and four years in which our country has endured a nationalistic, racist, misogynistic, proto-fascist wannabe despot. I was in the homestretch of my chemotherapy on November 3, 2016, when I cast my vote at the local library for Hillary Clinton, with my three-year-old daughter hanging from my shirttails as I filled in the ballot. I informed her, on our way home through the precipitous twilight, that when she awoke in the morning our country would have, for the first time in its history, a president who was a woman. (Well, we all know how that turned out.) In the January of the new president's inauguration, I was timidly venturing forth from the cave of my convalescence when I felt an overriding urge to reexamine and challenge who I was as a writer, just as the country's identity would be reexamined and challenged in the years ahead. This parallelism was never purposeful; indeed, I often felt incongruous—improper, somehow—swept along the rapids of civil upheaval while enjoying the respite of remission.

In 2019 my family and I spent a few months in London thanks to a TV production that had hired my wife to be funny. Returning to the UK felt almost like a homecoming. Not long before, my first poetry collection, as well as a play of mine, had garnered some friendly notice there, and for a few years I had cause to make easily a dozen long-haul visits for readings, literary festivals, theatre productions, etc. I thought I was receiving such a warm welcome because, in comparison to American readers and audiences, the British are known to be more admiring of political poems and plays, especially poems and plays that happen to be critical of the US. (If this was true several years ago, I doubt it is the case now.) It also seems to me that the British have always been more accepting than Americans of writers who write in various genres, for reasons I won't attempt to untangle here. Or my admittedly minor successes in the UK were simply the result of timing, luck, circumstance—in other words a mystery. Regardless, all my felicitous transatlantic traveling came to a halt with my wife's diagnosis in 2015, and mine soon after.

We understood our recent stay in the UK as a windfall in all kinds of ways, but also as an opportunity to escape the relentless unease at home—the ambiguity of our remissions, and the anxiety tearing through our culture. As foreigners largely ignorant of the details, we were able to observe with cool curiosity the tumult of Brexit. Rising nationalism and regressive conservatism including, bizarrely, a Trumpian yellow-crested buffoon as Prime Minister, made the UK seem like a universe uncomfortably parallel to the one we had just left. We did what we could to ration the news from both countries, opting instead to inhabit, for the moment, our fantasy of literary Hampstead. We were indulging ourselves, we knew, but without too much guilt, because during the year and a half of our cancer treatments we had wanted nothing more than to get as far away as we could from our home in Los Angeles—our literal home, our house and sickbed—and to begin again someplace untainted (to us), a celebrated locale where we could more easily imagine the resumption of joy after the entr'acte of catastrophe.

We had been planning another sojourn in London with the new year for a new season of my wife's comedy—until yesterday, when the UK announced a second national lockdown. So, once again, I don't know if I will be back there anytime soon. There is so much that—like everybody—I just don't know. I don't know if the theatre as an art and industry will survive, at least in its familiar forms—and much of what's familiar in the theatre ought not to survive (p. 78). I don't know how harrowingly the pandemic, with a quarter million Americans dead and cases surging as I write, will progress this winter until ultimately, hopefully, with the deus ex machina of effective vaccines, it resolves in the spring or summer. I have no idea who will win the US presidential election in a few days. When I have finished with this preface perhaps I will know something.

*

Politics is theatre. And vice versa, insofar as plays and musicals question or—more likely, if they hope to make any money—reinforce political assumptions and trends.

Many like to say that a politician's words and policies are 'only theatre', an insulting phrase to showfolk as it implies that our art is disingenuous and inconsequential. But we live in an age in which leaders and the laws they enact are both performative *and* consequential. Their version of political theatre causes actual pain for actual people. Above all my goal in writing these essays is to articulate why the theatre and writing for it matters. To elucidate how the endeavor of serious theatre-making is not frivolous or ornamental, but an existential struggle to justify, comprehend, and even alter who we are.

I was awake most of last night and am watching the counting of ballots today. This will take a while. Waiting for election results feels a lot like waiting for the doctor to call with results of a scan or biopsy. But it's only politics, not cancer. I am relieved to record here that the current regime has likely lost.

Granted, little has been settled; elections, like dramaturgical crises, serve mainly to rearrange and set the scene for the drama to come. There will be recounts and lawsuits, more lies and denial, unrest and violence, attempted coups and who knows what else. But I am happy to steer this preface toward a happy ending—a rare enough event in any realistic drama, on- or offstage.

Many are disappointed that victory has not been

immediately unequivocal. What they had hoped for was a silencing rebuke of Trump and his tens of millions of reality-averse supporters. But I am content—no, elated—to see my country slip through the net of annihilation. To me there is no such thing as a lesser survival. With a win comes the chance for more life, and for that most valued of theatrical currencies—change.

For years now I have been thinking of this little book as a 'part one.' Such an ambition implies that a book twice or three times its length might encompass every aspect of the playwright's craft and my long-standing obsession with it. But the theatre is immense, larger anyway than any single, solitary life. These hundred or so pages, then, I offer as the start of a mostly personal story that I hope desperately to augment as long as I live, as long as that may be, knowing that of course the story never ends, for when it does we are really turning the page on another beginning.

Time and the Theatre

2017

A play is a story that happens. It's here—this moment, this accretion of moments onstage—before it's gone.

I prefer 'moments' because rarely do we retain a play's words, no matter how lyrically or pithily or wittily they've been uttered. We revel in, hold on to, and carry with us these moments that moved us—out of ourselves and into the present.

Many years ago, though not so many years, I sat in a room and listened to a writer speak. I considered him old; I was not yet thirty. The writer was Barry Hannah, and he was somewhere in his sixties—an age far, far over my horizon. He was meant to deliver a lecture about the craft of writing fiction. As far as I can remember, he spoke mostly of his recent treatment for colon cancer. I can still see him: the casual way he leaned back in his chair in a toppled column of sunlight, describing for us the morning when he woke to a vision of Jesus at the foot of his hospital bed.

I can't quote any of the lecture. What I remember was

how that day, those moments, moved me deeply. Made me feel embarrassed—for what? For him? Me? I was awake. I was scared. I wondered, *Is* this a craft lecture? Now I know it was.

About eighteen months ago, six months after my wife had been diagnosed with stage 2B breast cancer, I was diagnosed with stage 4 colon cancer with metastasis to the liver. Luckily—I want to say miraculously—the metastasis consisted of two small lesions located in a resectable portion of my liver. I was given a very small chance for survival, smaller for a cure, but they did use the word 'cure' (medically speaking one is not considered cured until ten years have passed without recurrence). My liver surgeon remarked offhand that a few years ago I would have had, at most, six months to live.

First, they removed seven inches of my descending colon, then somehow stitched me back together without the need for a colostomy bag. They took 10 percent of my bladder for safe measure. Then I received four months of intensive chemotherapy; they 'hit me with everything', as my oncologist liked to phrase it, because I was relatively young and could withstand it. Then my liver was resected, only about 15 percent of it, as the chemotherapy had shrunk those two lesions substantially, reducing the smaller tumor to just a smudge of scar tissue. They nipped out my gallbladder—again, just to be safe. Then two more months of chemo. My treatment, as had been promised, was over by Christmas.

According to recent scans and blood tests, I currently

reside in the 'no evidence of disease' category, a term that has more or less replaced the apparently out-of-vogue 'remission', which is fine with me as the latter has always implied a mere respite from the disease anyway.

Chris Shinn is a playwright about my age. He is currently NED after not one but two bouts of Ewing's sarcoma, a cancer usually afflicting children. When I reached out to him after my diagnosis for some sort of solace—advice, maybe—he said, among other things, 'Bet on yourself.' And why not? We are playwrights after all; we're accustomed to thinking, Perhaps my next play will be a hit, win a prize, move to Broadway or the West End, or at least move somebody deeply.

But I'm realistic too. 'No evidence' means no evidence now, which is of course all we always have.

Physicists, philosophers, and my Hollywood psychic will tell you: only this moment exists. Easy for them to say; we don't know what 'now' is. William James defined it as the 'short duration of which we are immediately and incessantly sensible'. I read somewhere that the present moment is twenty-five syllables long: a respectable sentence. Dramaturgically speaking, the now is what theatre practitioners refer to as a 'beat'.

A beat is a unit of action. One beat begins when (and where, on the page) the previous beat ends. This juncture is change, and change is what keeps the audience awake. Change crackles, casts light, smolders, fizzles—explodes.

—

When I was six years old, my father raised a glass of cheap champagne as midnight approached on New Year's Eve and bellowed, 'Say goodbye to the '70s!' I fell to pieces sobbing. He took pity on me (this is my only memory of him loving me) and whisked me off to bed, where he read me *The Sorcerer's Apprentice*, just as the '80s came sweeping in.

Like everybody, I presume, I have always been terrified of time. Its loss. This is why, I am sure, I write plays, an activity in which I can control, at least in my imagination, the passing of time and, more importantly, what change it contains.

I remember learning as if it were a Masonic secret that a page of script in 'standard playwriting format' works out to about a minute of stage time. Ninety pages runs ninety minutes. Infinite time and space, bound within this wooden, highly flammable rectangle of paper. As the Buddha might as well have said: 'O for a muse of fire.'

Because plays are temporal and fleeting, most of the time they are disposable.

As a student I could be glib about this, and pompous too. The theatre's perishability was a major point in its favor, an almost sacred characteristic that contrasted mightily with the tawdry mercantilism of film and TV. Literature too. Film and video and paper degrade in time, but theatre like prayer is magic.

You can buy plays, but it takes a critically and commercially successful production to ensure a script's publication (most play publishers make their money from licensing performances, not selling books). And plays are painful to read by design, as they require so much of our imagination. Plays have to be seen to be believed.

Because an extraordinary play happens purely in the present, watching it—and performing it—is an experience of both joy and sorrow. And I don't mean simply those comic and tragic masks: I mean the joy I felt as a young actor, standing offstage waiting to step into the light. I'd been a shy child, though for some reason my family and friends thought otherwise (I was a good actor). I was drawn to the stage precisely because I was terrified—to stand, to move, to speak in front of strangers. I wanted to prove to myself that I was somebody other than who I was. Backstage with my nose to the black velvet, heart pounding, mouth parching, I'd soothe myself, intoning in a whisper like an incantation: 'You're alive, you're alive, you're alive . . .' till I heard my cue and made my entrance.

If this feeling of pure presence is not joy, then I don't know what is.

Regarding the sorrow of the theatrical now: these moments of joy have to end. And some plays and productions are bad, or good but taxing. And there is grief in the days and weeks after a closing performance. Relief too. Not unlike a life.

Plays are shaped out of the mystery of empathy. The playwright's joy is the actors' joy is the audience's joy;

that's how things are meant to unfold. All those other emotions too. But joy foremost—in the awareness, however conscious, of our privilege to inhabit this moment together in a theater, however grand, or some dusty black box somewhere—doesn't matter—sharing our individual allotments of life with a story that is happening right now, right before our eyes. The actors are here with us, spitting and aching, sweating and straining and at times transcending. The theatre is sacrifice: these tickets were expensive; the actors—and the playwright—are being paid practically nothing.

I have heard Paula Vogel say that as she matured she realized that concision in her plays was important because our days are numbered; what an honor (and responsibility) it is for the playwright that an audience is giving not minutes but hours of their lives, and asking the play to fill it with meaning. And not wasting time means for the playwright not wasting time on the page with repetitions and redundancies and tangents. Everything in a play should happen for the first and last time.

There's an old backstage joke about old audiences that any given performance could be their last. But it's the same predicament for everybody, regardless of age. All of our clocks are ticking.

And speaking of counting: some say each of us has a certain numbers of heartbeats. Others, the optimists, and I count myself in their camp, say that we will enjoy more beats the more we use our hearts. So, playwrights: give us more life—give us a thrill. Which means thrill yourself while writing. You are your first audience, and sometimes, sadly, your only audience.

As for young people: a bad play—boring, cloying, cringey—might very well keep them from darkening a theater's door for the rest of their days. So, for art's sake, think of the children.

My longtime (but still quite youthful) agent asked me recently, 'What will we do when all the Boomers are dead?' I think about this question frequently; I share it with you ambivalently. How I've longed for audiences of my own generation, those more likely to understand me, to share my confusions if nothing else. Every playwright knows that Saturday night's standing ovation unfailingly precedes the Sunday matinee's chorus of snoring and squealing hearing-aid feedback. (An aside: be skeptical of the popular young playwrights. Many are metaphorically tap-dancing at the old folks' home.)

But if you are efficient and precise with your dialogue, the escalating action of your highly personal conflicts, your ever-more revealing disclosures of character, the resonances and complexities of your unfolding themes, your audience—of all ages—will neither get ahead of you nor fall behind; thinking neither of their future ('When is this thing over?') nor their past ('Why did I say that at dinner?').

Like Samuel Beckett, like Caryl Churchill, your plays may get shorter the longer you are a writer; likewise each play as you write will shrink—'coalesce' or 'fuse' is probably better—from first to last draft. My plays tend to expand and contract with each successive draft, as if it's a breathing organism, until the text is 'set,' or beyond my control, ready to be inhabited and interpreted by the speech and actions of the actors on opening night and for as long as the production may last.

When I was younger I wrote plays that tried to include everything. I suppose this was a Shakespearean ambition. But there's a reason the maximalist James Joyce wrote only one (not very good) play. Or as Pound said of his *Cantos*, 'I picked out this and that thing that interested me, and then jumbled them into a bag. But that's not the way to make a work of art.'

The more I write the less I include. I keep only what feels necessary, potent, dangerous; often what comes to feel obvious. I think, 'Why didn't I think of that before?' I try to ignore my notes and, frankly, the notes of most everybody else. Things that occur to me when I'm not writing will most likely be useless to me when I am writing.

My first 'finished' draft (number fifty? sixty?) is almost always a third too long, maybe longer. But day by day, beat by beat, I learn what doesn't belong. What is, again, repetitious or superfluous. This has little to do with short attention spans. This is how a story happens.

This is also why unfavorable theatre reviews, in print and in conversation, can be hostile if not abusive: we feel that the play has stolen hours of our lives. Our time on earth—and I say this personally, passionately now—is precious.

This is why audiences riot in the theater. Perhaps I'm mistaken, but do readers riot over novels and poems?

Seldom, I'd wager. But if booing and affronted exiting can be considered riotous then such behavior happens all the time in the theatre; I saw Harold Pinter walk out of a Neil LaBute premiere (the rumor was that he found the music oppressive). Some opinions are passive. If I may humbly brag: Alan Rickman slept through most of a play of mine.

When you or a loved one are gravely ill, you can't help but feel that now is undeniably and inescapably now. Nothing matters aside from doing everything you can, and then some, to keep her alive, to keep yourself alive—now into your shared, uncertain future . . .

You can't help but take things one day at a time, as they recommend in recovery. As I suppose I am—or hope I am—recovering. One moment. One beat at a time.

When one is gravely ill, anything can happen, and often does. In a play, anything can and *always* does. Must happen. Every moment—a potential calamity. We've all seen an actor go up on their lines. Disaster is beautiful. You can hear a pin drop.

*

Writers are fond of advising: 'Write as if you are dying.' The threat of death is meant to clarify.

This approach sounds well and good, but I'm here to tell you that it's difficult to do; I mean, writing this way isn't exactly fun. It's joyful, it's sorrowful. What did Rilke say? 'Every angel is terrifying.'

Nobody truly wants to write a play for an audience of the living when one is possibly not going to be around to watch it with them. I want to hear your applause. I want to sit on the aisle in the back row or up in the balcony (or 'the gods', as they used to say) and watch my play 'work'—move you and wake you to the present moment of my story, the way my story as I wrote it woke me to the present moment of my life.

Writers advise you to write this way, with the skull upon your desk, if you will, because you may, in such a state, through such a frame of mind, write with your eyes open.

My friend Paul Watson, a recently retired war reporter, has been telling me for years now some version of how 'it bugs me to the core that people don't notice how quickly we die. Whether we're driving home from work, or sunbathing on a beach in Phuket, and a wave comes in and just keeps on coming . . .'

Or this: a friend of a friend was honeymooning not long ago; it was the day after the wedding and he was driving with his new wife when a spider crawled onto his shoulder, causing him to swerve minutely into an oncoming bus. The bride somehow survived.

One must write while awake to life, to death, in a state of barely controlled terror, but more importantly one's characters should be terrified too. They should fear for their lives.

But life, like art, is subjective. I'm paraphrasing

Chekhov when he said something like: 'I want to write plays where people are sharing a civilized meal, and one person's life is coming together while another's is falling apart.'

'The graceful adventure of conversation' is how I remember Borges—definitely not a playwright—putting it.

Terror lies in the eye of the beholder, so one must frighten oneself first, must 'write toward danger', as Romulus Linney once declared, in a lecture that I happened to witness while an epic thunderstorm raged outside the lecture hall's windows.

Because I have written mainly dramas, and documentary and memoir plays, I may sound as if I'm shilling for more of the same. But the best comedy is dangerous (I have this on authority from my professionally comedic wife) as it satirizes the powerful and assails shibboleths. There's a healing honesty in comedy too, in telling the truth about our vulnerabilities and fears and shames.

The playwright Joe Orton was rehearsing the premiere of his seminal farce *Loot,* in which the titular stolen goods have been stashed inside a casket that is supposed to contain a character's dead mother; the corpse is stuffed instead in a cupboard. Hijinks ensue, her body's tossed around onstage, undressed, done up as a dressmaker's dummy; at some point her glass eye pops loose and rolls around—in and out of hands and, if I recall, a mouth. But the play wasn't working in rehearsal; it just wasn't funny. So one morning Orton brought in his dead mother's dentures and asked a particularly problematic cast member to hold out his hand. He placed the well-worn prosthetic teeth in the center of the actor's sweaty palm: 'These are my dead mother's teeth,' and the actor reacted with a queasy mixture of revulsion and anger. 'That's what's missing from your performance,' Orton said. And by all accounts the play got better.

I have wanted to wake up for a long time. Many of my plays began with the command, figuratively and in one instance literally—'Wake up!' It's a cinematic commonplace: all those bedside alarms, our protagonists waking to the stories that will change their lives forever.

But my urge to see and say things as they are was counterbalanced by my fear of life, by the muddle of my anxiety and ego. My repression. I simultaneously hid and revealed myself in my plays. I gravitated at first toward historical epics, where time in its grandest sense could be stage-managed, and where the casts were large and the ideas larger. My props—I'm serious—propagated out of control. I camouflaged myself in clutter.

I was drawn to ghost stories too: for the ready metaphor of child abuse, or so I discovered with distance (and therapy), but also because my true self was present like a ghost in my plays.

I used to think that all good plays were haunted, or they were hauntings at least in terms of their performance. When I was new to New York City I wanted to start a theatre company called the Dead Theatre. Partly this was a joke, as in, Okay, fine, the theatre's dead; it's been dead a while yet we're a theatre and here we are. But also: Let's do what the dead do well, then. Haunt. Let's step out of the wings of the past, out of the individual and the cultural unconscious, and remind ourselves and our audience of something unsettling and unsettled that needs to be confronted and, if possible, set right. So I liked forgotten stories. Or, better yet, unknowable stories that alluded to unspeakable truths.

But I was still, myself, half-hidden. Or I was creatively somnambulistic. Remember: I am you; the playwright is the audience. By trying to wake you up, I was trying to wake myself up.

We all wake up, again and again. It's a dramaturgical fantasy that our lives can change fundamentally in a climactic instant. Trauma reverberates backward and forward in time.

When as a boy I witnessed my brother throw himself out the window of our attic (or the immediate aftermath of his self-defenestration, really); when as a young man I left my agoraphobic family for Ireland with only an overstuffed pack on my back; when I was disowned by my family more than a decade ago, for reasons I'll never fully fathom; when my wife Jessica texted me the results of her biopsy—I was in the middle of auditions for a play of mine in Manhattan and she was home in LA—'it is cancer' (her cancer); when six months later I awoke from twilight sedation to the news of a tumor the size of a softball . . .

In all these cases the thought occurred to me, concurrent with my panic and dread, that I was receiving a gift, if only I could survive it.

And each time I woke up, I wrote better. Some of it was too raw to be pleasing, but I found I could write more forcefully. This isn't just boasting—I can't claim that anybody else felt the same way about my writing, if they were paying attention at all. My new authority was something I sensed in the moments of writing, what Barry Hannah called 'the party at the typewriter', which is all we have anyway as writers, the rest being not our business—because it *is* business.

Lately I have wanted to write plays between you and me. Happening now, in this room; sometimes in a fictional setting, sometimes with two actors playing a plethora of characters. But always and intimately two people in one place: two-in-one and a one-place that is changeable, vertiginous, with an audience of whomever might show up. No sets, or not much . No props, if you can imagine. No miming—please. Lights and sound still belong—as storytelling tools, but also because these elements are suggestive. We are theatrically inside my head—why pretend otherwise?—a head in the midst of waking up.

It's trauma, of course, that wakes us. Disasters, private and public—illnesses, divorces, earthquakes, elections, or the joyful catastrophes of falling in love, realizing a dream, having a child—force change, or create the desire to change.

As in war, I suspect, so it is in the sickroom: senses heighten. Details emerge. Every leaf on a tree, it has been said. In my case it was smell. Like a superpower, or a symptom of pregnancy, I was almost canine for a while. It was hard to bear, and it's only slightly abated. My new plays are noticeably smelly.

In the midst of trauma everything means something. Signs and symbols appear. You've noticed them before, you're a writer, but now you see them everywhere. You take comfort in the symbolic meaning of passing pest-control and plumbing trucks. The numbers thirteen and fourteen. Spiders as a metaphor for chemo (let them crawl through the house of your body and do their dark work). Yes, as Viktor Frankl noted while surviving Auschwitz: even birds.

So you pray. For angels. You meet some. That male nurse who caught you as you fell the first morning when you tried to walk after surgery. The nurse who embraced you as you sobbed and told you that her daughter was born in 1973, just like you, and she has a rare cancer and 'she's still here'.

These are dramatic moments that meant something, must mean something.

Naturally the past seeps in. So be it. Your life flashes before your eyes, but in slow motion, over weeks and months—a year. You may succumb to writing memoir, before the tide recedes, before you've recovered or run out of time.

This summer is also that summer. Yesterday is today. I

sat on that bench in Cork City in Ireland scribbling poems in my notebook, just as I sit on this bench in Kenmare in County Kerry scribbling these words. Or—I am revising these paragraphs now on a grassy hill in New Hampshire in the village where, almost to the day, I was married eleven years earlier.

I remember my first writers' conference easily: one-on-one, a decorated novelist who'd read my short story suggested I should try writing plays instead. (Why did I believe him? —*Did* I believe him?) My best friend's mother, whom I loved more than my own, was dying back home in a hospital bed in her living room of a recurrence of breast cancer. The week before, she had beckoned me to bend and kiss her, and when I did she asked if I would become a poet and I answered emphatically 'Yes,' I already was: I was going to a writers' conference, wasn't I?

But eventually trauma ends, somehow. You will know you're feeling better when you feel you want to write.

You are rebounding, on your own two feet, when you find yourself envying other writers again, just a bit. You may feel let down. You worry again that your writing is no good. You crave accolades and applause, again. You desire.

And you desire because you are healing. You are astonished! Yet now you want to know—need to know—what has it all been for?

*

'You have peered behind the curtain,' they say (they seem to like to say). It's a platitude but I enjoy it for its theatrical implications. The sick have seen the ropes and pulleys, the backs of the scenery flats, the stagehands bustling amid sawdust and loose screws and rodent droppings. We have glimpsed something of how it all works, this performance of living.

My former collaborator Roberto Flores, a Chicano activist and anarchist, said it to me: *Behind the curtain.* He almost died a decade ago from hepatitis C followed by liver cancer, but at the last moment a family friend's death and organ donation saved him. The donor had been a strapping teen, and Beto is small; his new liver juts from his side, under his arm like a football.

Paul Watson the war reporter, when he learned of my cancer diagnosis, emailed me: 'Writer write thyself. No doubt you will see things only you can tell, with your words.' The idea is common: almost dying should make us wiser. Kinder. 'A deep distress hath humanised my Soul'—Wordsworth, remember?

We have all peered behind the curtain, in the moments and weeks and years of our cataclysms; we should tell the world what we have seen. What we are beginning to learn.

I have changed. Though like all change I know it's temporary.

My bladder's smaller. My liver's grown back. Parts of us regenerate, others don't.

My hands and feet are numb from neuropathy from the

chemo. But they've been waking up. I've been told this can take a year or more. Some feeling never comes back.

I've learned to be less careful. I was a dedicated hand-washer for years and look where that got me.

As a writer I was perfectionistic—an aesthetic hand-washer—but I am less so, much less so now. Perfection is seductive, but messes have more life.

Overall I'm less afraid.

Of premieres, for example. Still, I don't want to see that evening's performance or, worse yet, chat with you at the after-party. It's no insult to you or to my colleagues, but my work, as they say, is done here.

I'm less scared to give readings or lectures; I don't need a drink, before or after.

I'm less nervous to meet you in life. The awkward thing said and unsaid, yours and mine—I just let it fly, let it lie. Doesn't bother me much.

I'm less scared of rejection. I mean, who cares? I want to eat, sure; I need a job, some respect. But I almost died; I could be about to die again. What does it matter if somebody I don't know doesn't care, for whatever reason, for what I've written?

I lied: rejection still hurts. But less so, much less so now . . .

I'm grateful more often. Bewildered constantly. It's too early to feel guilty. I distinguish less between what I live and what I write.

I cry more. I look forward to crying, though I don't let my young daughter see.

She is three years old and right now squealing with delight 'Sandpipers! Sandpipers!' along the beach in Caherdaniel, on a misty late-June morning, with her mother following a few steps behind, when two years ago I thought her mother would die. When I know she will, one day, as I will. But now we may have longer together than we thought. With my lower back seized from driving the perilously twisting lanes of rural Ireland, I lie on a bed of rock above the cove, just as I lay in countless gurneys over the last eighteen months, wheeled into operating rooms and the spinning, droning orifices of CT and MRI scans; I now allow others to care for me, when I have to.

I have learned that I feel annoyed to be called brave. As an artist and as a survivor.

My wife feels much the same, having been public lately about her cancer and treatment, and basing a season of her own TV show on the ordeal. Perhaps we're modest or in denial. Or we are annoyed because we've had no choice—the choice was whether or not to give in and give up. But we were given hope by our doctors, and before that we'd been given our daughter.

Maybe we just don't want you to feel sorry for us—your commiserating, well-meaning frown-smiles. We don't want the presumed distance between us reinforced.

When people say we have been brave, what they mean is that we have been brave to talk and write about it. Cancer. Or in my previous plays writing about war and about the mental illness and abuse in my family: 'How brave,' many have said. Some adding, 'I couldn't do what you do.' Meaning: *I couldn't—wouldn't—reveal what you choose to reveal.*

Far be it from me to judge anybody's suffering and what they choose to do with it. Many times I've wished I'd kept my mouth shut, as a writer, about many things. A therapist once told me that I have trouble distinguishing secrecy from privacy, and she was right. She's still right.

But vulnerability is a taboo, and one I believe every playwright should violate—for ourselves, for our characters, and for the audience. This is unnatural, of course. We fear that in our weakened state we will be exploited, seized and preyed upon. In the many months of my treatment I was irrationally frightened as I hobbled along the bucolic lanes of my Southern Californian neighborhood; it would have been easy to be mugged, to be murdered, I felt. I could have been blown over by an ill-timed puff of wind.

And yet I've always believed that it is my obligation as a writer—my calling, I am apt to call it in my more priestly moods—to try to tell the truth about that which is most difficult to be truthful about. To tell others the truth, as skillfully as possible. To make art out of pain. To heal.

We are running out of time. 'Running', notice, not walking; plays (and all stories, and lives) sprint through their conclusions.

But wait—that's it? Time moves slowly when we're young, when we're bored and waiting. Time flies as we age, acts two three four of our lives . . . Time ceases to exist when you're having fun, and by 'fun' I mean, again, joy-sorrow-terror. Presence.

You have heard it said of Shakespeare that his tragedies are over when everybody's dead, his comedies when everybody's wed. Though a wedding is a kind of death, as it starts the story of a new life together; and there are survivors onstage at the end of *Romeo & Juliet* and *Hamlet*, etc., to make sense, and poetry, out of what we've witnessed together.

Dramaturgs will say that one has reached the end when the problem of the play has been solved, when the protagonist's conflict has been settled. There's nothing left that *has* to happen. Our time out of time has run out, and we in the audience are given back to ourselves and our changing bodies—the ever-revising stories of who we think we are.

Endings that feel like beginnings are profound. And if not profound then accurate. As Sam Shepard said: 'The most authentic endings are the ones which are already revolving towards another beginning.' I like that: 'revolving'. We know that the story continues elsewhere, with other characters, without us watching.

So take heart. Another play will make you laugh like this one, cry like that; many will bore, disgust, and—if you are lucky—enrage you. The best, that is the most life-like play, will do all these things and more over the rollicking course of its very limited engagement.

What's that ancient adage about never dipping your toe in the same river twice? The river's always changing. But so are we.

It's a luxury to stand beside the river. As if we are not in it. The young, the healthy, enjoy this delusion. They watch the afflicted characters in their stories rush by. The playwright luxuriates this way too, sitting upon the shore composing, as does the audience in the moments in which they are compelled, within the spell of the play.

We are all in the river, in actuality. Essentially we are the water.

Maybe this is not so much an examination of the playwright's craft as a description of where I have been living for a while now: between the graveyard and the river. As I have literally lived for a week while drafting many of these pages on the banks of an estuary on the southwestern coast of Ireland. The River Sheen on one side, like Time's river, and a famine graveyard just up the hill from me. Through one living room window I can see mossy Celtic crosses, one crowned with an almost full bottle of whiskey. A few years back I would have found my location unnerving. Now it is the skull upon my desk. Because I know that this is life: out the window on the other side of the living room my daughter runs in the grass above the glimmering Sheen.

Unspeakable: Speech Onstage

2018

I was standing in a mansion beside an old poet who sat in a chair like a throne. You know the place. We were waiting for the dinner gong; writers were drinking wine. He was a formidable and forbidding figure in most ways. We'd dined near each other along the interminable communal table many evenings that month, but I hadn't yet found the courage. It could have been the wine but I said, 'You teach at this school. I went to this same school. Do you happen to know this writer I know?' He fixed me in a sidelong squint: 'Quit bugging me, man.'

I was speechless. The Supreme Playwright might well have written 'awkward pause,' or a Pinteresque 'silence,' in the script of our minuscule drama. The unspeakable yawned between us as I exited the mansion without dinner, pursued by my shame.

What makes a play play?

Other ways of writing can tell stories of struggle and change like prose; are stirring and linguistically pleasurable like poetry. Ask any actor—ask Hamlet and he'll tell you: what makes a play playable is speaking the speech.

And not 'a speech' necessarily (more of that soon) but words as they are spoken: fractured and failing yet striving and flailing toward the mouth's translation of the heart's tongue.

As I once heard Terrence McNally explain, when we write speech we are really writing behavior. For what we say is arguably the most conspicuous thing we do. And what we do as playwrights is fashion words for a myopic medium. Film and television, theatre's well-compensated cousins, communicate in close-ups on screens as big as houses, or discreet like decks of cards that we hold to our faces in bed at night: every twitch and flicker of mind made transparent. Onstage the most charismatic actor stands only about three hands high, or peanut-sized, depending on what we've paid for our seats. We see plays primarily with our ears.

To write a play is to write literally what is said. Writing what-is-done is at best presumptuous and, in the worst cases, cinematic. Acting notes in a script are insulting; parenthetically describing your characters' inner lives is uncouth if not verboten. Stage directions should be written modestly and with regret. (Entrances and exits, kissing and killing excepted.)

I used to write lots of short stories. Maybe I will again. But at some point I grew weary of description—writing and, I confess, reading it. I wanted my stories to happen like life, and in plays I found a form that required—no, demanded—the barest essentials: where and when we are, how we got here and how we will go.

When I'm writing well I don't envision my plays so much as overhear them. I read the words on the page, but I try not to. I don't stage my plays in my mind except vaguely, as if in shapes and colors, movement and dimension. Because the theatre is that most practical of magics, words must reach the rear of the balcony where the face of the actor has become a blur.

So playwrights listen. It is a cliché of our craft: we imagine we are taking dictation. The better we know our characters then the clearer we will hear them speak. We find ourselves distracted and intrigued by what they say—what it is they have to say.

Conversation isn't dialogue, though. It is a beginning. It is a beginner's exercise to transcribe a meal with friends; assuredly as a performance it will bore. If your meal has been extraordinary—a breakup or a seduction—enacting its transcription will still probably produce a scene that's redundant and malformed, both underdeveloped and overelaborate.

By contrast, speech on stage is compressed and precise. Each line, theoretically each phrase or word, reveals something new, increments—or more—of plot or characterization or theme (in that order of efficacy) conveyed without patronizing or outpacing the audience, while allowing for laughs and gasps and utterly airless points of apprehension, and all this without shattering the illusion of reality, if our style is naturalism, or the reality of the illusion if something else.

What is the audience apprehending exactly? Alas, it's

hardly ever what's been said but the meaning: something true has transferred with the line—'on the line' is actors' lingo—but the truth is decidedly not the line. The truth in well-written speech is commonly and somewhat depressingly referred to as subtext.

I have been trying to avoid jargon for mostly aesthetic reasons. But subtext—let's get this out of the way—consists of objectives and motivations and stakes. These words are technical so I choose to speak when I can of the inarticulate, the unspoken and often unspeakable.

The unspeakable in life is easy—or easy to recognize. We read it, or try to read it, in conversation all the time. Because whoever says what we mean? Who truly knows what we mean and how best to express it? Who can be sure what others mean when they're trying to speak to you? When your doctor tells you 'fifty-fifty', he may mean survival rates are single digit. When your friend sees your play and says 'congratulations', she may mean she has despised it. We don't tend to trust people who speak in rehearsed, conclusive sentences and, God forbid, paragraphs—these are salespersons, politicians, TV news commentators. Most real conversation proceeds by hints and guesses, feints and dodges, implication and inference. As playwrights we don't so much write speech as improvise it, and then we craft it.

This is the reason almost every first draft (and third, and fifth) is overwritten. Maybe too much is happening, but usually it's all the talk that bloats and clogs. Too much of anything at the outset can be helpful, though; every tailor knows it's easier to cut cloth than to adhere it. But there is an art to cutting.

I spend many of my days at my desk deleting dialogue. Because I am inveterately cautious I like to bracket first by hand, then strikethrough, then remove words when I am sure; and by decluttering my speech of the words that don't need to be spoken—that cannot be spoken—I find I am loosing, if you will, a more living speech. Actors in rehearsal may help a new play along with, 'Can I cut this line and instead be it or do it? If I step from Line A to Line C, or leap to D or F, without these intermediate and preparatory words and phrases, will the speech still make sense? Will it make *more* sense? Will the speech—will I, the actor—come alive?'

A living speech infused with the unspeakable will sound naturalistic. Neither expressive nor impressive, naturalism is the illusion of life and still the style of the popular, unpretentious play.

But even naturalistic plays arrive at moments of clarity in which characters say exactly what they mean. If these words are earned—fomented in crisis and issued without thinking—then the audience will feel pierced by truth. If unearned then they will feel cheated; such speech sounds too perfect, that is to say 'on the nose'—like a punch on the nose, its canniness offends.

What of speech without the unspeakable? Flesh without soul? Is it truly such a sin? Like lust it is tempting and dangerous. In melodrama, and melodrama's laughing shadow farce, speech is too good to be true—yet satisfyingly so, when it's written well. A bargain has been struck: the audience foregoes intrigue for the spectacle of opera or slapstick. And yet a spectacle must beguile consistently, in exponential permutations of pathos or amusement, or we will quickly grow tired of life lived against the flats.

Let us now look more closely at the surface of the page:

Speech is speakable. Actors call these lines 'actable'. The words sound right because they feel right in the mouth and lungs (to say nothing of other body parts).

Creative spelling and compounding and capitalization for effect have been known to occur. Italics are most common for emphasis, but overemphasizing *too* frequently can read as amateurish or downright domineering. Some playwrights underline these words, perhaps in homage to that relic, the typewriter, and a few renegades are bold enough to **boldface**. Speech in ALL CAPS will read like a shout or scream or shriek and is best reserved for wacky comedies and Grand Guignol.

The comma is special. We playwrights must forget what we've been taught because speech is far from prose. Which is not to say that commas in scripts mean less—they mean more: rhythm, rest, hesitation, breath. And what the breath reveals.

(Our freewheeling use of commas is one of many reasons why writers of other genres look at us, and what we write, with both admiration and distrust.)

Parentheticals in dialogue are unusual, but some playwrights use them anyway, to suggest what a character is about to say or wants to say but can't.

Semicolons are literary; but, curiously, colons can be conversational: they seem to say, *Wait till you hear this!* Exclamation points should be used reasonably unless the speaker is feeling unreasonably.

Ellipses and em dashes are indispensable, if too convenient. They're the wider cracks in speech where the subtext streams out. Ellipses sink our speakers' words and thoughts . . . inward; em dashes imply thought and speech casting out—reaching—racing toward meaning. Em dashes—at all costs not to be confused with en dashes or hyphens—can suggest your ums and ers without the need to so crudely spell out these filled micro-pauses. Fragments for the most part play naturalistically. A slash in the line may indicate the point at which the next speaker begins to speak in overlapping dialogue (though we overlap much more in life than we can afford to onstage). Columns are sometimes utilized for extended runs of simultaneous speech for two or three or more characters.

A paragraph break can denote a beat, which is not necessarily the same as paragraphing in prose, but most playwrights eschew paragraphs and simply embed the stage direction 'beat' or 'pause' or 'silence' like rivets in the fabric of speech. A beat isn't always a pause—characters may experience a shift in understanding or desire without taking the time to reflect. And a changeless pause or silence is still dramatic: the tension will vibrate through the absence.

Pity the poor souls who, like me, choose to write their plays in verse. I haven't always done this but I do so now—for selfish reasons mainly. For the focus it affords me, the superstition of syllables, the compression and precision, the unspeakable ironies insinuated almost imperceptibly with the hitch of a line break. I don't care if an audience calls it poetry. Many playwrights arrange their speech in a kind of free verse, so that patterns on the page might inflect all kinds of intangibles like pace and style of playing, supple fluctuations of character and tone. There is no good reason other than difficulty why this kind of poetic (or 'heightened' or 'stylized') speech can't be actable.

Actors and directors and producers will look for 'a lot of white' on the page, because brief lines of dialogue consisting of sentence fragments and words—toppling through blank negative space—promise to play quickly, thrillingly, while paragraphs of dialogue are typically hard to perform, and harder to sit through. Audiences take pleasure in talk that plays like tennis—at least at first; extended volleys can grow tedious and vacuous. And occasionally a dense play is terrific. These rare wordy scripts may appear impenetrable on the page, but in their playing their speech becomes porous, riven with tantalizing gaps that provide actor and audience alike with electrifying glimpses of the inarticulate.

There are tricks on the surface of the page, of course, regarding speech. Comedy has its catchphrases, for example. If you are new to playwriting you will find yourself developing a retentive ear; dining alone in restaurants, eavesdropping remorselessly, sifting conversation for the tics and tells that give us all away. The grosser of these verbal mannerisms transcribed on the page and reproduced onstage will elicit easy recognition—*Yes, I know who that is.* The man of a certain age who habitually responds, 'Actually . . .' The woman of a certain age fond of euphemistically 'cutting the umbilical cord'. (Many years ago while teaching I noticed how I would automatically preface the explication of some element of craft with the phrase, 'There's a way in which . . .' Evidently some part of me wanted to evade responsibility for what is, after all, mostly taste and bias.) These artifacts of speech may help locate your characters in history, region, or culture. I refrain from writing in 'dialect', speech rendered phonetically on the page, because I don't wish to reduce my characters to caricature or worse. I try to set down the right words, correctly spelled, in their authentic order.

A few other practical suggestions: pronouns in naturalistic speech are often implied; relatedly, don't fake urgency by stating a character's name repeatedly; try to make your *wells* and *you knows* mean something; never echo a line or phrase at the end of a scene for dramatic effect.

I'll repeat that: Never echo a line or phrase at the end of a scene for dramatic effect. It's cheap.

As for the problem of speeches, the secret about writing a monologue is that there is no secret: a monologue is simply a dialogue when one character won't shut up. Can't shut up. But the listener is still present in the page. The listener interrupts repeatedly, albeit wordlessly. The listener is an equal partner in the moment-to-moment story of the speech.

Some find it useful to separate monologue into three kinds: (1) the conventional monologue, when a character speaks to another character (even if the listener is invisible to the audience, or exists only in the speaker's imagination); (2) the soliloquy, when the listener happens to be also the speaker; and (3) direct audience address, which is pretty much what it says it is. But a vital play is multifarious; these categories, if they exist at all, comingle.

The conventional monologue is easiest to write and to perform. These are the speeches actors prefer to use for auditions because they are comparatively straightforward. The soliloquy is seldom seen and heard in modern plays because it's not naturalistic, except under extreme circumstances of psychic pressure.

In direct address, the speaker essentially narrates and, like voiceover in film, a little narration goes a long way. It may help the audience imprint, if you will, on the narrator as the protagonist, particularly in a memory play. Longer, recurring speeches delivered to the audience are confiding, confessional. This kind of monologue is prevalent these days, despite its usual lack of dramatic friction, and can impart a slack theatricality to an otherwise televisual play. Still, an exciting direct address is conflicted. Stand-up comedy, where the comic strives to 'kill' without 'dying' onstage, is a useful example of the entertaining danger of direct address.

Let us imagine I am reading these words, performing, as one does, in front of an audience. I must earn your attention with the potency of my ideas and language and storytelling. Inject a bit of conflict though, between these words and the listeners, between me and you, and things might get a bit more interesting. A heckler—an estranged and outraged relation?—disrupts us. A medical emergency in the audience or up here at the lectern. Or say you happen to know—or I happen to let slip—that the success or failure of this lecture could cost me my job. Maybe you've heard I need the money for an operation. Somebody of influence clambers noisily for the exit. I veer off script and find myself extemporizing wildly. My performance will come alive.

Or without resorting to such cheap theatrics, all I have to do to make my speech more dangerous is to make it more personal.

*

In the middle of writing this I underwent a procedure. It had been a year and a half since I finished cancer treatment, and two years since my wife finished hers. In my paper gown and turquoise hospital socks, with the curtain rolled tight around me, I laid there listening to the other patients in the prep room behind their curtains conversing with their nurses. So many things said struck my ears vividly: 'I'm from White Plains. No, above the Bronx. I used to take the BQE to White Castle.

I liked jogging across the Washington Bridge.' 'My wife's Nadine. I told her, You go to a eatery [note: 'a eatery'; dialogue is deliciously ungrammatical]. Don't wait here.' 'Hello, I'm Mr. Meeks. Gloria's just a friend. I don't have much family left here in Los Angeles.' All I needed were the voices, really just the words, to imagine these people—not what they looked like but who they truly were or might have been. Perhaps these specks of speech dazzled me so brightly, just moments before receiving the blessed lethe of the Propofol syringe, because I was afraid and hopeful. As my characters are when they speak. As I am when I write.

And what I am afraid of is silence. The best plays I've written, or the plays I've most enjoyed writing, have needed little or no cajoling. Their voices came unbidden, in whispers that grew insistently into a companionship of months or years.

Admittedly my reception is irregular. I transcribe in fits and spurts. I speak for my characters as a placeholder; I grow confused. How do I know I'm hearing their voices and not my own? This is a delicate question. But do I like this talk, or bit of it, a lot? Does it impress me? Is it, as they say, 'well-written'? Well then I must delete it. If a character says and keeps saying what I mean for him to say then I should disappear him from the play altogether. For some reason people still like to counsel young writers to 'find their voice'; for me the practice of playwriting has always involved doing everything I can to lose my voice.

My characters still sound like me, I know. I don't think

it can be helped. If not the way I speak, then the way I think and feel. We contain multitudes, but they are kindred.

As a boy I was spooked by the story of the prophet Samuel. The seer. Though probably he should have been deemed the listener, for as a boy himself of eleven or twelve he heard God's small, still voice in the dark of the night calling his name. When he answered, 'Here I am,' his story could begin.

If you are regularly hearing voices then you are schizophrenic. But many of us have heard a voice or two in our time. While wide awake. My erstwhile mentor Charles Mee was a writer and editor of historical nonfiction, when in middle age, sitting in the audience with his daughters at the theatre as the house lights dimmed, he heard a voice behind him say: 'This is the real world.' He turned around to see who it was, but nobody was there. Considering that he had never heard voices before, he figured he should pay attention to this one, so he quit his job and started writing plays.

The voice I heard was both in my head and out. I was a few months free of college, anguishing alone in a narrow room in Cork City, in a narrow apartment above the bloody-mouthed drunks and sooty seagulls and black swans drifting along the emerald-churning, bacterial River Lee. I was pining for my home in New York, for the young woman I'd eventually marry—even for the family that abused me—when I heard plainly: 'Why do you ignore the doors?' The voice was male and female and neither. Ageless. I have tried to pass through every door since, especially when I don't know what I may find on the other side.

During my nine months of cancer treatment I did not, somewhat to my dismay, hear a voice. Perhaps I did not need to. Or I could not bear to.

But voices of a less psychotic variety have always defined my creativity. Early on I discovered I was a gifted impersonator, in person and on paper. As several therapists over the years have asserted: I lack firm boundaries. Voices get under my skin.

The first voice was my mother's. I would listen to nursery rhymes between her legs on the stairs, or on her lap in her rocking chair in the mornings when the rest of the world was busy elsewhere with school and work. Mother Goose. Humpty Dumpty, all the King's horses and lions and unicorns. Britannia: her fabled forebears. Poetry was likely inculcated here.

And when she wasn't reading to me she was talking to me. She could talk nonstop. Telling stories of her gothically unhappy childhood, complaining about my siblings and my father.

When did my mother's relentless talk first strike me as crazy? Long before I learned the word 'logorrhea', before I'd read Molly Bloom's soliloquy or seen Katherine Hepburn's spectral Mary Tyrone, I learned from my pathologically loquacious mother that conversation obfuscates more often than it explicates or reveals, and that, when it does come, revelation is usually accidental. This knowledge made me a dramatist for my pains, and a difficult one at that, or so I have been told on occasion.

As a boy I found I could imitate my mother's speech easily, in conversation but also in my head. And not just her voice but others, real and imagined. Hunkered in the bath I would argue with myself as if virtuosically, sustaining every dialogue in my mind's ear—phrases and words whirling in a seemingly inexhaustible vortex. Not unlike hearing voices. But her voice was always most distinct. I still write my mother in the countless characters that derive from her, though I haven't heard her speak in more than a decade, and she is fading.

Her brother Bobby was twelve years old when he was diagnosed with schizophrenia. Obeying the voices in his head, he set their mansion in Scarsdale, New York, on fire. Their father, a shirt manufacturer in Manhattan, had the money to send him away to be raised by a family of devout Christians in Calgary, near a doctor famous, and ultimately infamous, for claiming he could cure schizophrenics with massive doses of niacin. Needless to say, Bobby remained insane. My mother never saw her brother again.

Sometimes the phone would ring on my birthday and if I answered an old woman would speak: 'Danny? This is your Nana Ruth'—the grandmother I'd never met. She sounded like my mother, the same eerie, vacant chattiness. 'You and I were both born on the same day! Did you know that? And *my* mother too!' Then she'd put Uncle Bobby on. She was visiting him in Calgary, an annual pilgrimage after her messy divorce from my grandfather in the sixties. 'Hi,' he'd say dopily, like a kid; had he been lobotomized? The timing for that historically was right. 'Do you like baseball?' and I'd have to admit that I did indeed like baseball, so much so that I hoped to one day play for the Mets, but by then he would have hung up.

When I was young and feeling myself capable of poems like an oracle at Delphi or a young Dylan—Thomas or Bob, I loved them both—I'd worry that these words came to me the way a voice might tell a schizophrenic to set his family's house on fire. My labile mind aflame, I felt elated, energized; the gods spoke through my mortal mouth and told me things I knew without knowing. The otherworld and the subconscious were synonymous, I realized then.

My mother must have been terrified. My hypochondria, just one manifestation of my undiagnosed (and therefore untreated) obsessive-compulsive disorder, bordered on the delusional: I'd contracted AIDS by brushing against a stranger at the bookstore, I was certain; that stitch in my side was irrefutably lung cancer. There are moments I still wonder about my sanity, like when I am writing well.

I have spent ten years writing about, and in a peculiar way with, the war reporter Paul Watson. I think of him now as a friend—in some complicated ways like family. As he stood amid an angry mob in the streets of Mogadishu in 1993, readying to photograph the desecrated remains of a US Army Ranger, he heard the voice of the dead man speak both in his head and out: 'If you do this, I will own you forever.' Paul snapped the shutter anyway, again and again, capturing a series of gruesome images that would win him the Pulitzer Prize and alter the course of American history for a generation to come. I too have felt haunted by this soldier; I never heard his voice, but I have sensed his presence over my shoulder as I wrote at my desk, felt his gaze from the dark balcony at performances of my play about Paul. I don't know how the ghost, if he exists, feels about what I have written. He may be displeased. But his voice is secondary; I took on Paul's voice when I took on Paul's story. As Paul is 'owned' by the trauma he witnessed and suffered, so I am owned—that is, altered irrevocably—by Paul's trauma.

Several years ago I went through a period of susceptibility to psychics. I was as interested in their charlatanism as I was in the possibility of any supernatural reality. Spiritualists are at their very least theatrical, which is undeniably the case with my Hollywood psychic, who lives in Burbank and claims to have been raised in bleakest Appalachia. He is flamboyant, his hair a frosty caramel and his accent cornpone. I know it's a ready alibi, but I find him most sympathetic when he describes his voices—of the dead, of angels, of his spirit guide Spencer—as imperfectly heard. His skill varies from day to day. He needs rest, calm, focus. He must take care of his instrument. He is an artist.

For—make no mistake—there is a whiff of the occult about what playwrights do. And believe it or not I resist it: that way lies not so much madness as solipsism. If you cede too much control to your voices, whoever or whatever they are, they may lead you away from reality. Like elemental spirits they are tricksters. But even those readers not spiritually inclined may find the psychological explanation sufficient: emotion suppressed will find its strange and startling voice.

*

I was twelve that winter when my brother tried to kill himself by leaping from our attic window. I saw him stumbling around the side of the house in the snow in the moments after. I found his suicide note upstairs that read, 'Dear Mom, looks like you'll get that playroom you've always wanted', and, regrettably, later that night I handed my mother the paper. She collapsed crying in my arms and whispered in my ear, 'This is a secret we will take to our graves.'

I knew in that moment she was wrong. In order to save myself—and her—I would have to betray her.

Every family is a cult, or a culture at least unto itself. Ours was a tyranny in which we were not allowed to speak our minds, because our minds were teeming with words in protest of our treatment at the hands of confused and cruel parents. No, protest wasn't our goal—love was. Compassion.

Displacing what I wanted to say, and what my subconscious needed to say, into the mouths of other, imagined people—this adaptation allowed me to thrive. At least for a while.

Of course I was afraid. The few times my parents read or saw my plays I worried: *Will they hear me in these voices? Will they hear themselves?* 'You've always liked to make a scene,' my father said after my first production, and that's all he said. I was safe, for now.

For the stage is a displacement that offers transcendence. With the actors as surrogates and the page the public square, the play may be a festival or an execution; the danger is real, but so is the reward of the audience's compassion.

Earlier I suggested that plays should lack the playwright's voice. But talented playwrights and their plays do possess a kind of voice. We know it when we hear it, and we won't hear it in the speech. Our voice is the voices we hear and how we hear them.

So we listen for what's unspoken in our culture, and it won't be what the audience wants to hear. But we use our art to make them hear it. They will disagree, because they see things differently; because they don't yet know how they feel; because they don't want to feel. The truthful play you write will make you allies and, if you are doing it right, enemies. You will hinder your career by offending those who have risen in their ranks by institutional and commercial rather than artistic acumen.

We are living through unspeakable history. The foundational poison in America has found its full flower again. The reactionaries are ascendant and their cruelty is reflexive because kindness is called weakness in their church of

Mammon. Real is fake and the lie is king. Disparagement unto silence is only one strategy. They are working tirelessly to stifle and extinguish our smallest, stillest voices.

Why did I begin with a memory of shame? When an aged, esteemed poet suggested that I 'quit bugging him', and I did so because I didn't matter, I was a youthful thirty and the wrong genre. I was just a bug bothering him. And I am still stung. Though I forgive his annoyance now: life can seem too brief for small talk with strangers. He was unwell—he died not long after. I almost respect him now for speaking his mind then.

But I wish in that moment I had spoken my mind in response. Not to wound him but to answer his real speech with mine. For by speaking the unspeakable we may find ourselves conversing freely, creatively. We may listen.

Surviving Conflict

2019

I am often confused, having been abused as a child, as to why I choose to spend my life writing about conflict. You would think that as an adult I would want to run as far away from conflict as possible, and in many ways I have done just that. I work alone. When my five-year-old tantrums—thankfully a rare event, and almost always for good reason—I want nothing more than to fix things quickly, or better yet to prevent her upset with more supple parenting. I am incorrigibly soft-spoken. When I teach I try not to persuade. I have been accused of appeasement on many fronts. At dinner parties I do my best to help everybody get along.

A psychotherapist would say—as, full disclosure, many have said—that I choose to spend my life writing about conflict precisely because of the conflict of my childhood; I am compulsively striving to control, even to master an abstracted conflict in my plays in the hope of quelling not only the humiliation of past abuse but the resounding, self-destructive directives in my psyche. All this is true. But as usual the explanation cannot solve the problem.

—

Scriptwriters believe in the inciting incident, that precise moment in our first five or ten pages where and when the conflict that is our story begins. Perhaps it's fair to think of the following paragraphs as an elucidation of a few inciting incidents in the never-ending conflict of my personal dramaturgy.

Like most adults in therapy, I believe my parents could have used some therapy themselves. I have had to conjecture, for the sake of my own mental health, that my mother suffered from something called borderline personality disorder. She never got herself diagnosed but she checks enough boxes: splitting (also known as black-and-white thinking, and devil-god characterizing of loved ones); a ferocious if delusional fear of abandonment; uncontrollably intense emotions disproportionate to events and situations . . . Borderline people, to be flip about it, are dramatic.

Theirs is a disorder of perceiving conflict, and they overreact with such resentment and rage that they invariably end up creating the very conflict that so terrorizes them. If you were raised by a borderline parent then you have come back from the war—in other words, survived into adulthood—attentive to the merest hint of an incipient quarrel. You are anxious. You are maybe a writer. You know in your heart, in your very cells, that the nature of conflict is fascinatingly relative—if conflict makes any sense at all.

If I had been his therapist (and he never had one, as far as

I know) I would have diagnosed my father with paranoid personality disorder, comorbid with schizoid personality disorder and autistic spectrum disorder, with a touch of psychopathy. Yet he was by far the less frightening parent, because mostly he ignored us, reading his science fiction and fantasy novels and watching TV (*Cops* was a perennial favorite). Living with him consisted of long bouts of boredom punctuated by his explosions of shouting and swearing and walls punched and dogs kicked; he only ever hit his children, to be fair, a few times. But we knew where we stood with the man—as far away as we could manage to stand, or bunkered in our bedrooms with our doors closed and books in front of our faces, for by avoiding him we hoped we could avoid his conflict. Both of my parents also exhibited florid symptoms of depression and anxiety—just to round out the sunny picture here. The anger of their children, it should almost go without saying, was verboten.

Like a victim of Stockholm syndrome it was easy for me as a child to sympathize with my parents, as they were abused themselves when young; but they didn't talk much about that—or at all, in my father's case. They weren't Roman Catholics or Latter-day Saints but they begat a lot of kids anyway—six of us, which was in itself probably abusive, considering our circumstances. And while we got along fairly well as siblings, we splintered and scattered into our various adulthoods like fugitives of a totalitarian regime, wanting next to nothing to do with each other because our memories were too painful, and the old ways of seeing and being ourselves in each other's presence too easily resumed.

It took me years to begin to understand why the theatre had drawn me inexorably toward it: here was a family to replace my family. Inside the theater my new family engaged in conflicts of story that resolved themselves artfully thanks to the alchemy of collaboration. Of course collaboration—with actors, directors, designers, dramaturgs, producers—creates its own kind of conflict behind the scenes: discord in the rehearsal room ('What's my objective?'—but more about that later) and the pressures of rewriting during workshops and as press night approaches. If we failed as a company—lackluster reviews, anemic ticket sales—I would feel that I had failed personally and existentially, and this feeling was dimly but deeply familiar.

*

What had my childhood taught me of conflict? That it is pervasive and incurable. That its origins are ancient and apocryphal and its only resolution is forbearance or martyrdom—strategies of avoidance.

As a young playwright I knew conflict *was* drama; all my teachers taught me so. But I wasn't always successful at writing it. My first plays were, at their best, absurd, approximating tragedy, and, at their worst, constituting a theatre of cruelty—even, God forbid, the antiplay. For all my sensitivity to conflict in my life, my plays were not conflicted enough. I was, like most sane people—perhaps more than sane people—conflict averse. I had yet to learn that conflict can be survived.

The teachers will teach you that your characters must be forced into conflict by what they do or what is done to them, and if they are not struggling to achieve, to change, to overcome in combat the wants and needs of other characters onstage with them, right now, then nothing much will happen. The drama does not occur. For while conflict in the theatre is made perceptible on the page by dialogue and stage directions, conflict itself is the substance of drama. Dramatists invent, build, structure conflict; we are conflict engineers.

These same teachers may teach you that conflict comes in three flavours: (1) the interpersonal, the most graspable category of conflict—for the characters, the dramatist, and the audience—because it is social and largely externalized; (2) an intrapersonal or inner conflict, illuminated by monologue and revelatory beats of interpersonal conflict; and (3) conflict between characters and forces in society—patriarchy, climate change, white supremacy; you can, if you want to sound like you have received an MFA, call this 'extra-personal' conflict.

Ordinarily one conflict will dominate. If this is a play about internal struggles, then odds are it's a full-length monologue or a solo show; if an external conflict is the play's raison d'être then it's agitprop or avowedly political theatre (or it's not a play at all but a blockbuster movie involving armies, superheroes, dragons). Most modern American theatre is, for better or worse, and for lots of reasons, concerned with the conversable struggles of close relationships.

Regardless of its focus, any worthwhile play involves many strains of struggle in concert, feeding and enforcing and intensifying each other. Inner conflicts pitch your characters into conflicts with other characters. Likewise the world around them influences your characters' private and relational conflicts in sometimes palpable, often subliminal ways. At the conclusion of the psychologically well-made play, the resolution of the exterior and interpersonal conflicts will have resolved the interior. If theirs is a truly happy ending then your characters will retire from the field of battle blissfully unconflicted in all spheres of life.

Actors talk (and talk, and I say this with love) about their intentions and motivations, or, more serviceably, their objectives, in the scene from moment to moment, or beat to beat, from inside the skins of their characters as they pursue their wants and needs. The other characters are likewise impelled by their own inner conflicts into conflicts with each other, and together these actions braid into the action and events of a play.

For all that, conflict will soon bore the audience if the playwright hasn't instilled a vivid sense of why said conflict matters. So, despite my distaste for the word, because it reminds me of Wall Street and equestrian contests, we must talk of stakes, of risk and cost, of the propulsive value and captivating power of a prize won or lost.

In tragedy and comedy (and the spectrum between) the stakes are life and death. But it is one of the playwright's most subtle skills to be able to convey the subjective nature of those stakes. And characters don't need to always know the reasons why they do what they do—they probably shouldn't know, most of the time—but the audience needs to learn what the playwright has already found out: the reasons for a character's behavior and why these reasons matter.

When structuring a play it's crucial to think in terms of a protagonist, or protagonists if we must. Love stories of any kind can be thought of as dual-protagonist stories in which our main characters share the same objective, that of consummation—though inner and external conflicts, as well as conflicts involving secondary and tertiary characters, will undoubtedly get in the way. Multi-protagonist plays, more elegantly referred to as ensemble plays, are the hardest to write; they can swell until they pop and dissipate with characters and their conflicts rambling and ranging every which way. Writing an ensemble play requires the deft knitting together of equally important conflicts that escalate and resonate and culminate with each other. An encompassing external conflict, often made manifest by a very real 'container' for the play's action—an ancestral estate with a cherry orchard in Russia, for example—may help the ensemble play cohere.

The modern American theatre seems to have lost interest in the traditional antagonist. Playwrights may write a relative or structural antagonist, a less sympathetic character whose wants and needs and actions conflict with what our protagonist is after; but the villain of old is scarce. It's as if neoliberal playwrights and their audiences believe that an antagonist is simply a protagonist that we have not yet fully understood.

But it behooves the playwright to remember, and to explore and exploit, the axiom that dramatic conflict is, in its purest form, the depiction of the struggle between good and evil. Us and them. Protagonist versus antagonist: Beowulf and Grendel, Cain and Abel; theirs is the essential human conflict. If we can believe in an enemy then our attention will be total.

Because in the end we all want to win—at least to survive. (The antagonist wants to win too, but we don't care.) Our objective in the audience is to vicariously achieve a resolution to the story that will feel like justice, maybe even like peace.

*

I never went to war. Trudging in the mass exodus through Chinatown on the morning of September 11th, 2001, away from the burning towers and the neighborhood where my girlfriend (and now wife) Jessica lived, I saw myself in my mind's eye someplace sunny and sandy like Afghanistan or Iraq, enlisted and fighting to defend my country. But I didn't enlist. Because I quickly found myself distrusting the objectives and actions of my country's response to the traumas of that day. Or I was afraid.

I come from a long line of physical cowards. The only warrior I'm aware of in my bloodline is the almost anonymously named John O'Brien who arrived in Manhattan fleeing the Irish famine, where he promptly exchanged his rags for a Union uniform, a hot meal and a rifle and a train ticket south. I don't know if he fought, or if he peeled potatoes behind the mess tent. All I know is that he survived, as evidenced by my existence.

While I have never been to war I have been writing about war through the eyes and ears and heart—through the protagonist, you could say—of Paul Watson. After hearing him on NPR interviewed about his forthcoming memoir, *Where War Lives*, I emailed Paul, vaguely seeking a creative collaboration. I didn't really know why I was reaching out to him, all I knew was that I felt unsettled by his story, and that investigating why would in some way constitute our prospective work together—should he reply. Thankfully, and with great consequence for me, he did.

This was 2007 and Paul had already spent almost twenty years reporting from war zones around the globe, beginning in South Africa during apartheid, followed by the Somali Civil War and the Rwandan genocide and the Balkans and our forever wars in Afghanistan and Iraq, and lastly, before his reluctant retirement in 2015, Syria. At the heart of Paul's story, from which I have so far derived two plays, two poetry collections, a libretto, and a failed TV pitch, is that series of photographs he took of an Army Ranger's defiled corpse in Mogadishu. These images shocked Americans and directly influenced the Clinton administration's decision to withdraw troops from Somalia, thereby emboldening an ascendant al-Qaeda with the lesson that a single well-publicized atrocity could defeat the world's greatest military power. And ever since that day Paul has lived in fear that he will be punished—drastically and irreparably—for what he perceives as the unforgivable moral transgression of taking part in a desecration by documenting it. When he was stoned and stabbed by a mob in Mosul in 2004, when two years ago he nearly succumbed to a bout of blood poisoning related to treatment for his polycystic kidney disease, Paul felt that judgment had come at last.

But the paradox of trauma and guilt aside, why was Paul drawn toward war to begin with? Perhaps because his father was a WWII vet who survived D-Day, only to die of polycystic kidney disease when Paul was two years old. Perhaps because Paul was born with just one hand and could never enlist himself, or because his brain chemistry was, for whatever reason, predisposed to depression, and the thrill of war provided a steady stream or cascade of dopamine that made him feel 'normal'. Whatever the reason, the young Paul Watson had an instinctive need to experience conflict—first as a freelance 'war tourist' in his college years, then as a hardcore adrenalin-junkie on the payroll of Hemingway's *Toronto Star*, then the *Los Angeles Times*. Paul has never hesitated to admit that he finds war thrilling.

Stories of war, too, can be thrilling, as everybody knows. Most war stories excite by lying about war, redacting chaos and carnage while hyperbolizing glory and valor. But the realistic war story invigorates too—by conveying the awful awareness of how violence casts reality in sharper relief, revealing to us a world more beautiful because it is more fragile and precarious than we had imagined. As Tim O'Brien writes of Vietnam in 'How to Tell a True War Story', something I have had the good fortune to hear him read in person with obvious emotion despite the decades since he wrote it: 'A true war story is never about war. It's about the special way that dawn spreads out on a river when you know you must cross the river and march into the mountains and do things you are afraid to do.'

I wanted to tell Paul Watson's story of a man haunted by war because I was haunted by my childhood. Survivors of child abuse often describe the homes they come from as war zones and their emergent psychologies as post-traumatically stressed into any number of disorders. When I began working with Paul I was physically free of my family but terrified in my freedom that I was cursed, that my independence would never be countenanced by the cosmos, and therefore, like Paul Watson, my judgment was fast approaching.

During an audience talkback after the performance of my first play about Paul, a discussion in which he and I had been rehashing much of the trauma in the play, a somewhat exasperated New Yorker raised his hand and asked us: 'But are you guys happy *now*?' I believe Paul answered Socratically—'Happy about what?'—which made everybody laugh uneasily; I said something sad about life always finding a way to present us with new conflicts, if we're just patient enough. What I didn't feel able to talk about publicly yet was that my wife had just been diagnosed with breast cancer; she was at home in California in the middle of her chemotherapy treatment. The next day I would rejoin her, and a few weeks later I would find myself diagnosed with cancer too.

I worried for a long time—I still worry—that the cancers came as retribution for the transgression of writing about Paul's transgression of taking his pictures of war. Paul feels significantly responsible for 9/11; the pulverized World Trade Center coated Jessica's apartment in Battery Park in dust, and surely despite HEPA filters we were inhaling that poison for months. It was September 11th, 2015, when Jessica discovered her lump. But I will never know the reasons why. Perhaps the cancers were punishment for the transgression of leaving my parents—I'd broken the Fifth Commandment, after all, or is it the Fourth?—though in truth they left me, or it was mutual. I had written so many ugly things about abuse and war over the years that I wanted nothing more now than to repent, to renounce what I'd written, never to write again if it meant that I could be forgiven and survive.

So: though I have never been to war I have been diagnosed with a metastatic colon cancer and have now lived two-

and-a-half years post-treatment without evidence of its presence in my body. I am classified as a survivor.

We know that we can survive many things in addition to war. Many or most readers of these words will have lived through bereavements, accidents, assaults. But the cancer-war analogy is common because cancer is common. Four out of ten of us receive a cancer diagnosis at some point in our lives, while only 8% of Americans are military veterans. But the bellicose metaphors are abundant and clichéd: we battle cancer; anybody with cancer is a warrior, an almost classical hero in a highest-of-stakes contest. And cancer is the arch-antagonist, a humanized yet inhumanly cruel adversary we must at all costs annihilate.

Some of the grosser similarities between cancer and war have to do with the horrors of the damaged body, the indignities of tubes and fluids, and the mutilations of life-extending and sometimes lifesaving surgeries.

Then there is the bombardment of radiation, and the chemical warfare of chemotherapy in which surgical masks are sometimes worn like Great War gasmasks, defending a compromised immunity from the mustard gas of everyday microbes and viruses. Cancer treatment is overall a long march; in its final months it can feel like trench warfare. We acquire a siege mentality. We are being held hostage and tortured.

And when cancer treatment is over, if we are lucky enough to return from the war, like veterans we find ourselves living in the aftermath with some degree of post-traumatic stress disorder. We too experience flashbacks and nightmares, repetitive and disquieting images, physical sensations that trigger, like a mild summer cold reminding us of the sandbagged limbs of the sickbed, or an after-dinner mint like a madeleine moment sucking us back into the months when near-continuous minting was required to counteract the nauseating taste of our own chemo-scoured tongues.

Despite our survival we wonder why the bullet of cancer hit us at all, and what we could have done to sidestep it. So we sidestep now: anything vaguely carcinogenic, but thinking magically we avoid also certain people and places, music and colors and styles of clothing that somehow remind us of the illness. We isolate ourselves, 'popping' our mental corners with defenses drawn, hypervigilant always to any possible symptom of recurrence.

PTSD from cancer can create conflict with coworkers, with friends and lovers and spouses through irritability and outsized anger. If I were more reckless I would reveal more here; let us just say that survivors fight with those they love because we cannot very satisfyingly fight with cancer. We are alive, at least for now, yet we find ourselves making a mess of our rescued lives.

Many survivors of both war and cancer may succumb to the life-and-death intrapersonal conflict that is suicide. Paul Watson has said that when his PTSD was at its untreated worst he would choose, again and again, to return to war zones in a half-passive attempt to get himself killed; he lacked the courage, he said, to do it for himself. Thankfully my brain is wired more for strenuous anxiety than despair; when I was languishing in the POW camp of my treatment a doctor, ticking through bullet points, asked if I was experiencing any 'thoughts of self-harm' and I was baffled: 'No, no'—I nearly shouted—'I want to *live*.'

My wife and I employ the cancer-war analogy frequently. We have wished aloud that we were survivors of an actual war because, we suppose, military veterans aren't tormented by the possibility that they could be redeployed back to hell at any moment. But of course that's not how PTSD works for anybody.

In our most private moments we may even miss the war because we seemed to know then what mattered: this moment, the love given and received within this moment, the beauty and pleasure to be imbibed with no thought or emotion greater than gratitude. We hoped then only to suvive the conflict of cancer so that we might inhabit more such moments in the future—any future.

And when by some miracle of medicine or fortune or God we find we have survived months, then years, post-treatment into a future in which we are living in Hampstead in London, thanks to my wife's latest acting gig, and I am receiving 'in the post' a literary journal from Boston containing poems I wrote four years ago while she was convalescing in bed in the morning post-mastectomy; and I go running in the afternoon in a heath not unlike the fire trails of the domain of Sewanee, Tennessee, another place where I felt optimistic; and I am collecting our pigeon-chasing, boisterous, somehow-almost-six-year-old daughter in her pale blue gingham uniform at the wrought-iron gate of a centuries-old church—then I know that I have been delivered back into the world but the world is changed. Or I am changed: a race apart, only another survivor can understand where I have been and who I am now. If I have withstood cancer then surely I can weather a rejection, a review. At other times I know I am letting myself down. Having gotten through all that, why am I tangled again in the old concerns, the petty doubts and rivalries, the frontal lobe? Why is the world less beautiful again? Is it because I feel safe?

Now, there are countless good reasons why the comparison of cancer to war will rankle and offend and here are just a few: nobody enlists for cancer; the vast majority of soldiers are young while most cancer patients are middle-aged or older (though obviously it's not solely soldiers who are devastated by war); the cancer patient is not required to commit state-sanctioned murder.

The analogy also implies that those who have survived cancer have somehow fought more valiantly, been more tactical or religious or 'positive', than those who have not survived. It is only a short leap to believe that those who are stricken with cancer must have done something to deserve it. When I was newly diagnosed, a Russian acupuncturist in Venice Beach informed me that my cancer was caused by my unexpressed anger (my conflict aversion?); I told her to shove it and slammed her office door on my way out, before a single needle of hers had pierced my skin. Such victim-blaming might be forgivable in reference to dedicated smokers, or Instagrammers vacationing in Chernobyl or Fukushima, but a quick tour of the pediatric cancer ward should cure anybody of the notion that cancer makes much sense. Like war its causes are manifold and overdetermined and undeterminable and anyway far more complex than any one of our singular lives.

So the metaphor is flawed; yet it can be therapeutic, even vivifying. I *feel* that I fought in a war, and I have returned with new knowledge. What should I do, then, with what I have learned?

*

Or more germane to the subject here: How did the conflict of cancer change how I write?

A belated disclaimer: I don't know if any of my ideas about conflict and story have matured in any substantive way, or if I have simply come through the fire, so to speak, with my aesthetics annealed. Perhaps I am the writer I was always going to become, given enough time and trauma.

But here is what I do differently now: I try to write as forthrightly and explicitly as I can about war and cancer but also suffering more broadly. I choose to ally myself with my subjects in the struggle of their stories as I have been accompanied and succored in my struggle by the stories of others. I participate in the ugliness in my stories because I know it's not ugliness I'm after but the high-relief beauty of Tim O'Brien's dawn spreading out across a river, the river of time we are all walking beside, knowing that sooner or later each and every one of us will have to march into the mountains and do the thing we are most afraid to do.

I wish to write now about only that which is high-stakes for me—that is, what matters to me and what matters is what scares me, infuriates me, disturbs me; what matters is what I am trying to figure out about life while there is life. My objective as the protagonist-writer has never been clearer. And I know what shouldn't matter—the creaturely demands of my ego like affirmation, acclaim, the vanishingly minor fame or fortune to which a writer may aspire—because when I could only manage to climb the stairs once a day at most, when sitting up in bed took too much effort, I didn't care what others thought of me and my work, and I strive to preserve this indifference. I cling most dearly in my recovery to the compassion—for myself and for others—that my illness awoke.

I write slower now because what's the rush? I write as fast as I can because what are we waiting for? I don't write for anybody, other than my wife and daughter, because I know it's possible I won't be around to see what I've written produced or published or in any way 'received'. A deadline means something completely different now.

I feel braver. Before cancer I was researching the Sandy Hook school shooting but couldn't quite face it; now I am writing the play because how can I not as a father with a child in America? It is a choice I make with trepidation; I would like to turn away, to write about pleasanter subjects. Some primitive part of me doesn't want to type these very words you are reading, as if committing the words 'school shooting' and 'metastatic' and 'retribution' to the page could somehow invite more misery. But another thing I know now is that none of us can hide.

If you take my advice—if any of this is in fact advice—I don't know if your writing will improve. I doubt what you write will become more marketable. A lot of people won't care about what you care about, or they won't care for the way you see and tell it. The world is busy with misery, and human beings can only bear so much reality—in their entertainment especially. The reality of any conflict will always be a hard sell.

As alluded to earlier, I have pitched only one television series in my career. Paul Watson and I concocted it together and we called it *The Zone*, which, I concede now in retrospect, is also the name of a fad low-carb diet. Our *Zone* endeavored to tell the documentary-style saga of Western journalists covering the war in Syria, and we imagined that with each new season our setting would pan around the globe to different war zones—Yemen, Libya, Ukraine, Somalia. We spent months preparing, developing a lengthy treatment of characters and their storylines, and weeks 'taking meetings' at all the 'prestige' networks, but in the end our pitch failed. It failed to sell for a variety of reasons, not the least of which being that the war in Syria had already failed as a narrative for the American audience. Just when the infotainment conglomerates thought they had identified the Syrian National Front as our protagonist, al-Nusra, also known as al-Qaeda in Syria, arrived on the scene and muddied everybody's sympathies; then ISIS, then Russia . . . The Syria conflict was (and remains) a mess, a miasma of antagonists and victims, a story that resists packaging as either entertainment or foreign policy.

Conflict that makes money must be presented as bluntly us-against-them. And I'm not just talking about theatre, film, TV; in the US alone war is a trillion-dollar industry. The line between entertainment and politics has been perforated for a while now, but the Trump administration's dominant political gambit has always been brazen deceit. We are lied to regarding our government's racist policy of 'family separation' and other brutalities committed against asylum seekers from Mexico, Central and South America. We are lied to about the presence and virulence in our country of racism and misogyny, trans- and homophobia.

And we are fed fictions meant to compel and impel us toward war, and more war, with Iran, North Korea, China (the list goes on). As Vice-President Pence addressed West Point cadets at their graduation in 2019: 'It is a virtual certainty that you will fight on a battlefield for America at some point in your life.' In other words, war is (always) coming—against 'Islamic terrorists', in Pence's words, but also Venezuela as '[s]ome of you may even be called upon to serve in this hemisphere'. Also at West Point, Bush the Second said much the same in 2002, setting the scene for the disastrous and ongoing drama of our felonious invasion of Iraq. Johnson lied about the Gulf of Tonkin, McKinley about the sinking of the USS *Maine* . . . History is made by political leaders who are willing and able to harness humanity's biological imperative for high-stakes drama.

This is why Paul Watson took his photograph that day in Mogadishu in 1993: The Pentagon was lying when they denied on numerous occasions that the bodies of American soldiers had been desecrated in the weeks prior, and they were able to get away with the lie because Paul hadn't provided any photographic evidence—yet. If the true story of what was happening on the ground in Mogadishu were known, the US intervention in Somalia would have appalled the average voter. Policy would have changed, lives would have been saved. So Paul told the truth with his art, with his photograph, which is why I believe that, despite his guilt, he did the right thing.

There is another kind of conflict in storytelling, intangible yet arguably most vital: conflict between the story you tell and the society in which you live.

I learned this early, and like many valuable lessons it begins in humiliation. I was telling some joke over and over, as children do, until my father far above me snapped: 'Shut up, Danny. It's not funny anymore.'

Years later, after my older brother had tried to kill himself, we would all eat dinner together (something we hardly ever did before) because my mother had gleaned from the parenting books that children need a 'stable family unit'.

So our dining room table became nightly a stultifying lie of normality. For the truth was that Mother despised how Father chewed: too much and too loudly; how he hunched to his plate and picked at the iceberg lettuce with his fork. My brother's lubricious mouth-sounds turned her stomach too. Father for his part ignored Mother down there at the foot of the table, unless it was to ask without looking, 'Where'd you get this meat?' (despite the fact that Mother often said she had only given us food poisoning once, when she—and we—were quite young so what was the big deal?) or to ridicule her for saying something 'idiotic'. He'd shake his head with disgust if she forgot, as she reliably did, to serve with the chicken his cranberry sauce, sloughed out of its tin can and sliced with a butter knife (only Father liked the stuff; my other older brother ate it but he ate anything). My older sister, home from college, would sit there inconsequentially nervous. My suicidal brother would say nothing while staring at nothing, and nothing was across the table where I would be sitting, so he stared at me or rather through me at the beige wallpaper with the wretchedly hateful expression of the incarcerated, answering any question lobbed his way with one word—one syllable if he could manage it. A thatch of dark chest hair sprouted in the gaping collar of his Izod; the seat of his jeans or shorts stuck lightly to the wooden chair when he fidgeted or stood, and we would snicker behind his back: such execrable hygiene!—which shouldn't have been funny because if he wasn't washing, his body or his clothes, then chances were high he was thinking about killing himself again. My little sister chirping beside Mother, my baby brother on Mother's other side refusing to eat, wisely . . . and all the while I was doing everything I could to undermine our father's authority with my jokes at his expense—jokes that were pointed and barbed when he had just barked something cruel about minorities or women or gays, or his wife and children. The closer I could cut to his bone the better—and the funnier. I made the long table laugh, or titter through tight lips, the whole captive audience of our large unhappy brood. My father, too, had to chuckle sometimes, as if he hadn't understood himself to be the butt of my joke, or he did understand but didn't have the wit to retaliate. I played the fool to his thick-headed Lear at the dining room table just as I would in my life moving forward as a writer, because he's right: it isn't funny anymore. It never was. It's life and death and I want to live.

Identity in Crisis

2020

Drama is the question of identity. We begin in a place of unknowing, our seats in the orchestra or mezzanine or nosebleeds, in the crepuscular hinge when house lights have dimmed and stage lights are rising, when we find ourselves wondering with a shiver of anticipation: Who are these people—these characters—before us? Who are we, for that matter, in the dimly anonymized, collectivized audience? And for the audience to wonder then the playwright must have questioned first: Who am I, or who do I believe myself to be, as I write this, and who will I have become when it's all over?

Most everybody has heard of 'negative capability': the concept that writers ought to be able to assimilate, saturate, transmigrate themselves into the that-ness of their subjects. 'Thou art that,' as the Upanishads would have it. Maybe it's a trick of the mind, but we playwrights tend to believe—we must believe—that in writing we give ourselves over to a state of excruciating, ecstatic empathy. We get this: we get inside their heads—the heads of our characters, though in rehearsal our aim is much the same with directors and actors (and designers and producers et al.) as we help them incarnate our characters. The dramatist's craft is practiced, spider-like, in the center of an elaborate web of empathies.

Theatre artists are fond of explaining that we do what we do 'in service of the character' (or 'of the story'—but there is no human story without lively and multitudinous characterizations). We make no judgements about them; or we accept our judgments reluctantly because we love our characters with something like agape or religious love. We love them because we know them or have come to know them, because we understand their motives and terrors, their appetites and aspirations; it's this very understanding that allows us to convey their humanness with both nuance and intricacy. The theatre is still, despite its many constraints—some would say because of these constraints—the storytelling arena in which complicated characters are most prized and praised.

There are two initial challenges for the playwright, as I see it, regarding the building of character: first, how to engender and nurture our embryonic characters in preparation for writing; then how to craft these characters with an eye always toward the page's eventual interpretation on the stage.

Our first task, the thrilling yet daunting confrontation with a nascent character's boundless possibility, is by necessity experimental. We must indulge ourselves; we should try to 'cultivate leisure,' as one of my more relaxed (read: tenured) mentors used to phrase it. (Easier said than done, I know, when in reality most of us are fighting tooth-and-nail for an hour or two, here and there, in which to dream.)

Many playwrights will go to great lengths to convince themselves of the reality of their unwritten characters. This research—for that's what it is—involves imagining most fully our protagonist (or protagonists) as we don't need to know our secondary or tertiary characters nearly as well. (Though why not attempt it? No actor wants to play a vague role, and no audience wants to watch its performance.) If you're writing a historical play then there's lots of reading to be done, interviews and travel (and grant-writing and -winning to pay for said travel). If your play is a docudrama or something akin, then there are many more interviews to be conducted, flesh-and-blood characters to be courted, 'life rights' to be hammered out and co-signed. These are the more time-consuming plays to write, as so much more information has to be sifted and sorted, discarded or dramatized.

But if you're conjuring your character out of thin air, wholly imagined, still you may find it beneficial to keep a journal, perhaps written in the voice of the character; playwrights have been known to also include drawings, photos, collages, quotations. Anything that sparks or feeds. Or if you're short on leisure time, write a biographical synopsis for your character. Create a musical playlist. Or if you're impatient or inspired, start running before you can walk in pursuit of your character's voice by cranking out copious scrolling monologues written without any real care or concern for its viability as drama. Most likely little of what's written like this will make its way verbatim into your finished play, but the characters may breathe for you and clear their throats—imaginary people that the playwright can begin to believe in.

We may not like to admit it, but often we're creating characters based on or inspired by those we know or have known. Ideally we love or have loved these specimens—ideal because we will know them well as we write them, or will be motivated by our love to draft and redraft in order to know them better. (And by love I mean yearning and heartbreak—the most useful kinds of love, dramatically speaking). Or your approach is more piecemeal: I've heard playwrights refer rather gruesomely to their characters as 'hamburger,' composed—or compounded—of bits and pieces of acquaintances and intimates, all mashed together and massaged into one meaty role. Modeling your characters on real people is arguably the easier and more natural place to start, though—fair warning—this technique may corrode your close relationships. So, whenever possible, try to write about people who don't read much or attend the theatre. This shouldn't be hard.

A character can, of course, be 'you.' A version of you, a stand-in, is sometimes referred to as the 'authorial spokesperson.' The accepted wisdom about such characters is that they will be poorly written: you, the playwright, likely lack the separation needed with which to see You, the character, from many perspectives. Blind spots abound. The character of You is reactive, passive, an observer or victim of the drama. When you have been displaced and disordered by the travails of your life, however, you may turn and marvel at who you once were, and in these circumstances writing a play about yourself is potentially a risk worth taking.

Regardless of exactly how we've begun, what are we hoping to glean from these preliminary fantasies? And how should we set about transforming our proto-personalities into convincing characters for the stage?

The rudimentary elements of our characters' identities belong, appropriately, on the 'character descriptions' page—things like age and occupation and a phrase or sentence about their temperaments; a thumbnail sketch. In the stage directions as the play unfolds we may permit ourselves the occasional descriptive elaboration: how our characters stand and sit and move, what they wear, their corpulence or leanness. But as the theatre is first and foremost an auditory art, it's dialogue that most effectively distinguishes our characters: what they say about themselves and others, and their idiomatic and idiosyncratic ways of saying it. In every aspect and from every angle the playwright is seeking to isolate and highlight the telltale expressions of their characters' broadest traits.

Superficialities alone, however, will render characters as types, and typical characters are boring or dehumanizing as stereotype. (Archetype is, in my opinion, just inoffensive stereotype.) If our aim is authentically dramatic, then we will communicate who our characters are by what they do—what they choose to do and what they cannot help but do—in a crisis.

What if 'who they truly are' is unlikable? Should playwrights fret about providing audiences with conventionally sympathetic characters, antagonists aside? It depends; we all like different things and people. Likability lies in the eye of the beholder (ditto 'relatability'). That said, charming and attractive and virtuous people do seem to go far in life, and their presence in your play as charming and attractive and virtuous characters may result in a likable—that is, well-received—stage production. Indeed, even the phrase 'having character' is used in life to connote admirable moral fiber. Just as we may say 'What a character!' of a person evincing an entertainingly weird charisma.

But we're wading in the shallows here. What instills empathy in your audience is how nakedly you reveal your characters' vulnerability as they grapple, with each other and with themselves, toward their consummations and failures; your audience needn't share your characters' values, or their lack thereof. We have all felt the thrill of identifying with an antihero or otherwise 'problematic' protagonist. What matters, again, is that the audience comes to know and understand your characters just as you, the playwright, have come to know and understand them in advance.

As a student I learned an exercise from Nilo Cruz that he'd learned from María Irene Fornés. Fold a sheet of loose-leaf in four, and in each quadrant answer the following prompts: What is your character's (1) most pressing hope, (2) most pressing fear, (3) most cherished memory, and (4) most cherished secret. Your answers will help you begin to envisage your character in suitably dramatic dimensions, while also strongly suggesting, before you've given any conscious thought to your plot, the structure of the play you are about to embark on. This exercise can be useful at any point in your process, by the way, despite its feeling reductive or artificial (because it is), insofar as it clarifies a murky character or reroutes a wayward plot. Personally I like how the twice-folded page evokes the crosshairs of a camera or a compass, aligning the playwright with the heart of the matter at your character's core.

Writing my first plays I was hampered by the suspicion that character was ultimately amorphous. If we could only strip away culture and more private, familial contexts, we would see—starkly and disconcertingly—the empty face behind the mask. Such a belief is probably forgivable in a young writer, and a young person, who didn't yet know who he was; but it led me to write plays in which my conflict unfastened my characters like so many Russian nesting dolls, revealing at the end of the evening little more than a well-lit void. I supposed I was saying something profound, approaching the mystical, but these plays weren't very satisfying to audiences, I don't think.

Because most audiences wants answers, they expect a solution to the mystery of character. We dramatists entice them with the recognition of themselves in our characters' words and deeds; once we've gained their trust, we beguile and entrance our audience with surprise: enchanting and insightful peculiarities and peccadillos, contradictory words and actions if our characters are to ripen with intrigue. The most thrilling surprise for an audience occurs when the play's conflict coerces a character into making an out-of-character choice that alters, sometimes radically, who they are to the audience, or—better yet—who they are to themselves. A revelation like this is worth the price of admission because the audience will have shared—voyeuristically, thankfully—in the character's reinvention of self.

Life is, of course, not neat. Our day-to-day is rarely revelatory. So let me conclude this opening salvo of dramaturgical assertions with a reminiscence of my father, as an illustration of the stubborn opacity of many real-life characters, but also as a bridge to an exploration of the notion of negative capability as a learned response to trauma. The memory I'm about to share isn't trauma but an instance—a sip—of the opposite. I'll confess it is a prose poem, entitled appropriately 'Character':

> Why do some heartbreaks persist? Like an August afternoon on the way home from a week's vacation in the Adirondacks when my father pulls over to the side of the road, a country dual carriageway, and parks upon the verge. He leaves us in the car, Mother up front and the litter of us sweating in back and

the nauseous wayback, as he strolls off alone along a footpath into the dappling shade of drowsy wood. How long has he been gone? Has he left our engine running? When at long last he returns he has filled his red stainless steel canteen with cold water from a spring. This must have been someplace from his childhood, where he and his cousins night-fished for electric eels. My father is not outdoorsy but there are reverberations of such manly—or boyish, at least—pursuits about him. He sits at the wheel in the car and drinks his water. So pure and painfully cold—I remember still, so he must have allowed us a sip, though that would have been out of character. Perhaps that's the reason I can't forget.

*

I have a theory, surely not original, or true, that most writers suffer a serious trauma around the age of twelve, just when our adolescent psychologies are swirling into configuration. My trauma at twelve, you will remember, was witnessing my seventeen-year-old brother's suicide attempt, or its immediate aftermath, when I happened to notice him staggering around the side of our house, seconds after he'd thrown himself from a window in our attic. In that instant, and in its countless repercussive waves that have rocked my life since, my sense of the world changed—not just how things worked, or didn't work, but how I was supposed to understand myself in the context of the world's chaos. Maybe my brother was himself a kind of chaos. Maybe I was.

Much later in my life I wrote my plays and poems about Paul Watson. He has frequently described his sense of disembodiment, as if he were standing outside himself, watching himself bend with his camera to his face to take those photographs of the fallen American soldier in Mogadishu. He remembers thinking: *You poor man, who are you?* In my interpretation of Paul's story the question was meant equally for himself: *Who am I to do something like this? To have something like this done to me? Who will I become when it's all over?*

Live long enough and you will fail, fall ill, lose, be harmed (or the ache begins earlier, if you're a believer in infant birth trauma, also known as the expulsion from the Garden), so hopefully you will agree that trauma at the very least disrupts identity, and recovery involves a fumbling toward the fashioning of a post-traumatic identity. A new character, you could say, defined at first by victimhood: one becomes a refugee, or a survivor of assault. These identities are often shameful (and concealed) because they have been imposed by the cruelty of others and imply the victim's weakness. My wife and I underwent this apocalyptic bewilderment when we were both diagnosed with cancer. We were no longer who we had known ourselves to be, youngish artists and new parents, but now instantly infirm, the unwitting protagonists in the sudden drama of our mortality.

But to return to my beginning: my brother's suicide

attempt was a symptom and not the disease; what he had done was pointedly a response to the abuse we were suffering as the children of mentally ill parents. Our father was thoroughly neglectful, as suggested by my prose poem. He was a static character in that he never changed. Or if he changed then we, the audience of his children, never noticed and never learned what made him tick: his fears and desires, his cherished memories and secrets. He remained locked to us like a stone.

My mother, on the other hand, was a dynamic character, capable of perplexing displays of approximate affection. But she'd survived a difficult childhood herself—an alcoholic mother who beat her, among other abuses (her cherished memories and secrets). She couldn't help but pass her pain along to us, we children rationalized, by way of her many manipulations and jealousies, delusions and lies.

My mother's undiagnosed borderline personality disorder is a condition characterized by, among other traits, a disturbance of identity. She never really seemed to know who she was. She needed her children to constantly affirm and reaffirm her life's ambition to be a good mother, which she evidently and tragically was not.

When anybody is abused they are being used to fulfill the objectives of the abuser. In my case my mother's needs were almost entirely emotional and practically impossible for a child to comprehend. But I had no choice: it was my role, as far back as I can remember, to comfort and console her, to buttress, when I could, her crumbling mentality. I was her favorite, her only friend, her confidant, her junior therapist, her emotionally incestuous lover. Any wish or request of my own was ignored or vehemently punished.

A mother's love cannot be surpassed, or so we are told; but rather it is the child, lacking power and freedom and knowledge of the world, who clings to the mother (and father) with the fiercer passion. My mother didn't love me, or she was incapable of it, so in response, and by necessity, my love for her was total and very nearly selfless—'nearly' because I possessed enough sanity to intuit that one day I would have to leave her.

But freedom was far in the future. To outlast I would have to outwit. I grew adept at surmising the obscurest subtexts in her speech and actions, her subtlest cues, the choices she did or did not make in a crisis (and our family was one unremitting crisis). I made myself permeable to her moods; I tried to become her—empathy my survival strategy. And she praised me for it: 'Danny, what a good listener you are . . .' especially in comparison with my taciturn brothers and father (I was unlike most males of the species was her implication). This solicitous negation of myself became my preferred method of interacting with a society that responded, like my mother, with admiration for my supposed politeness and consideration, my wisdom 'beyond my years'. When I wrote my first short stories my teachers were impressed by how wholeheartedly I was able to lose myself in my characters.

And all the while I was biding my time, planning my escape; or I was escaping already—step by step, semi-furtively—to school, to friends; and my mother took it badly. She liked to claim that she was just a little bit psychic, more so when it came to reading the minds of her children, and with this supernaturally acquired kompromat she would question and confound my adolescent subtexts at every turn. It didn't take long for me to realize that she wasn't reading my mind but my journal, in which I had been secreting, as one does, my most private thoughts, often in the form of bad poetry. She denied what she was doing when I confronted her. I didn't stop writing, but shrank myself down, made my handwriting small and smaller until my words were almost illegible; my poems became postmodern inscrutabilities.

Such enforced attention to another's inner life, not to mention an infestation of one's own, will hollow out a child. Like the emptiness I would envision at the core of my characters many years later, I feared as a boy the void inside me. I was incapable of identifying, much less exorcising, my grief and rage and shame. And if these emotions did not exist, I was learning, then in some sense I did not exist. I was unreal, invisible. I was a ghost.

*

And if not a ghost then a conduit, a channel, a medium for ghosts. I was used to being used, echoing my mother's voice but also absorbing her torturous character into my psyche where, commingled with my own inhibited desires, my distress manifested as handwashing (hypochondria) and praying (scrupulosity), among other neurotic outcries.

And most urgent in this panoply of maladjustment was my compulsion to write. I had no choice; it was a release, and a relief. Passive to my passion, I discovered that I could switch myself off, some awareness, and allow my characters to, as it were, transmit themselves through me. I wasn't always good at it, but when it happened I felt talented, and mildly crazy. Call it the muse, or the unconscious: whatever it was it was real to me.

Abused children will grow up to become adults who are uniquely susceptible to magical thinking. These are the true believers, zealots, conspiracy theorists, and very likely they've seen ghosts, or heard them, or sensed them. As a child I was repelled by anything remotely supernatural because the supernatural seemed too plausible (the New Testament with its crucifixions and resurrections gave me the heebie-jeebies). Perhaps this predisposition toward belief in the unseen is keenest in those whose injuries from childhood are psychological and therefore invisible. I was afraid of the so-called occult because I feared what was hidden inside me.

Some years into my playwriting vocation, I felt courageous enough to confront the occult by writing a play about the Fox Sisters of Hydesville, a desolate hamlet in western New York. I first read about them as a boy in my family's mold-speckled *Encyclopedia Britannica*, and their story of a haunting had haunted me ever since.

Maggie and Cathie Fox were 14 and 11, respectively, the winter of 1848 when they struck up conversation with the spirit of a murdered peddler, a traveling perfume-and-button salesman they called 'Mr. Splitfoot'. Supposedly buried in their dirt cellar, Splitfoot communicated via knocking or rapping sounds along the walls and floorboards of their dilapidated cabin. Within months the Fox girls—joined now by their stage-managing older sister, Leah, a single mother in nearby Rochester—had become fast-rising celebrities, holding séances in a hotel room in the Financial District of Manhattan (just around the corner from P. T. Barnum's American Museum), then touring up and down the Eastern Seaboard raking in the cash. The Fox Sisters are widely credited with inspiring the founding of the Modern Spiritualist Church, a loose affiliation of brick-and-mortar houses of worship still in existence today, and contributing charismatically to the rise of the long-lived culture and commerce of psychic phenomena, replete with table-tilting and 'Ouija' planchettes, ectoplasmic ejaculations, and levitating incandescent tin trumpets through which the dead might breathe, and clear their throats, then speak for themselves. In her older age Maggie Fox, penniless and ravaged by alcoholism, confessed it was all a runaway hoax: they had been surreptitiously bouncing apples tied to strings, popping the joints in their toes hidden beneath voluminous skirts, and other theatrical subterfuges to produce Mr. Splitfoot's discarnate dialogue. But her confession went unheeded as the movement moved and grew. The American Civil War, then the Great War in Europe, swelled the shores of the Summerland, as spiritualists refer to the afterlife, boosting demand among the living for this psychotherapy of modern necromancy. At the start of it all, though, the historical record suggests an impoverished household with an alcoholic father, among other family dysfunctions, so my play about the Fox Sisters was really about the flowering of art in the rocky soil of abuse. It was my most autobiographical play to date.

Spiritualism was undeniably a women's movement in an age when American women were barred from almost every egress of self-expression. Suffragettes and abolitionists were often spiritualists too—Susan B. Anthony and Sojourner Truth can be counted among the believers—and, not coincidentally, all three movements lay claim to western New York as their birthplace. The female medium of the spiritualist movement—and almost every medium was a woman—was creating, consciously or not, alternative selves, dramatis personae who could speak through her and for her, while she sat as if passive in dim drawing rooms or upright onstage in the otherworldly footlights, telling stories that the writer, if you will, could no longer repress.

Did I identify so closely with the characters of the Fox Sisters because my childhood abuse, my parents' suppression of my voice and agency, had made me feel feminine? Absolutely. I was unmanned, as a boy, then as a young man, by this affinity; but with it my facility for empathy, my negative capability, was beginning to bloom.

Many writers have famously drawn from the occult as the source of their creativity: the poets W. B. Yeats and

James Merrill spring to mind. I remember distinctly, at the age of fourteen, feeling like the envelope of my body was dissolving as I read Alice Walker's postscript to *The Color Purple*: 'I thank everyone in this book for coming. A.W., author and medium.' Is it possible, I wondered, that every writer is a medium?

One of the prime joys of writing is the temporary disintegration of the writer's sense of self. But I was also afraid: these characters, storm-thrashed and wind-driven to my door with grief and rage and ravenous need—where did they come from? From me? And writing plays frightened me uniquely. Maybe both the occult and the theatre are capable of eliciting shame and fear because a denial of one's true self is integral to the success of both illusions. Probably, in my case, I feared what my writing was liable to reveal about myself—to others and to myself.

The theatre has always been a clique of misfits. A safe harbor for outcasts. A circus for bookish types. I could go on, but instead let me speculate that theatre artists are people who don't quite know who we are. We are permeable, our boundaries unfixed. We are mimics and chameleons. And foremost in our cohort we must recognize the presence and contribution of the sexually conflicted, indeterminate, and alienated.

I definitely fit the bill. I did not feel typically masculine (though others seemed to be persuaded, more or less, by my performance of the role). The truth is that I had always believed myself to be somehow other, a hybrid third sex—a soothsaying Tiresias, or such was my ambition—

who, all the more bafflingly, dreamed of women. A Freudian would say that my father was too foreign, my mother too familiar. Or it's all down to genetics and hormones in the womb so who cares. I have wondered over the years if my proclivity to write in many genres, to blur or disregard genre when I can, when to do so feels genuine, might be a related trait—similar to my distrust of received styles and forms like naturalism and the well-made play, or sonnets and villanelles, for that matter; but these are questions for another day. In any case my sexual insecurity was alarming to me, and always a secret.

Inwardly in my teens and twenties I believed that all writers—probably all artists—were, in some essential way, omnisexual. As a generalization it is, I know, mistaken. What I mean to reveal is my magical thinking in assuming that any writer of talent possesses the ability to identify seamlessly with all characters of all genders and sexualities, ages and races and creeds. I believed fervently that theatre artists in particular, we exiles of blighted and blasted upbringings, who in our private lives so often paid the price of our ambivalences, nonetheless excelled in the arena of our craft. Our wound was our gift—the mythical consolation. We were nobody so that we could become everyone.

*

But I was wrong. We all know this now: we can't be everyone, and when we try we may offend. I have written my fair share of characters who were, at best, only metaphorically me: a gay fashion designer manqué dying of AIDS in 1990s Manhattan (my first full-length play); a middle-aged survivor of breast cancer haunted by her divorce and by an ambiguous angel in the backwoods of Tennessee; a Black American drama student visiting a comically(-intended) xenophobic pub-theatre in Cork City; a vaudeville sister act famous for the terribleness—and the racism and internalized misogyny—of their revue. I list these examples not to flagellate or expiate myself, but to acknowledge that in overreaching I no doubt exposed my limitations and biases.

So when writers ask me, and I ask myself, 'Should we stop creating characters who are very different from ourselves?'—my answer is yes. Let others write these characters and tell these stories. And don't fool yourself with the old excuse that you are 'giving a voice to the voiceless'; take a seat in the audience instead, and let the heretofore voiceless speak for themselves.

And when writers ask me, and I ask myself, 'Should we stop creating characters who are very different from ourselves?'—my answer is also no. Just write these characters well. Take responsibility and take care. Let doubt be your spur in making sure that you are depicting your characters with fairness and respect, accuracy, and the love of your most empathetic perception. Now, with our culture in the grips of seemingly intractable discord—this is precisely the moment when we cannot afford to give up on the dream of being one another.

My internal conflicts aside, I do not think one can write a diversity of characters without knowing who one truly is, where one comes from, how one's own character has been shaped. Perhaps one should write one's own story first and enlarge from there. So let me return again to my childhood story and the day and the hour in which the delusion of my negative capability was dispelled. Like most climactic episodes, on stage as in life, it happened accidentally and inevitably.

I was thirty-two, heading into my Jesus year. I was getting married. I should have seen it coming. My older brother was back in the hospital after another suicide attempt. My younger brother was graduating from college, and I was visiting for that, reclining in a lawn chair in their backyard when my father sat down beside me:

'What's wrong with you?'

I couldn't respond. 'There must be something terribly wrong,' he went on, 'the way you *look*.'

'How do I look?'

'Like you're homeless. Like you're insane.' Like my brother the chronically suicidal, he meant; and—just like that—I had become the family scapegoat.

He disapproved of my blue jeans, for starters. My untucked shirt. And that unkempt hair! That beard! It was disgusting and shameful—he was shouting—the way I *looked*.

'This is how I dress—who I am—' I was stammering to defend myself. My character. My tongue felt swollen, my limbs shrunken, vision tunneling . . .

'We're taking a walk,' he said, and he stood up.

'No.'

'We're taking a walk—you and me.' It was a threat.

I'd been to therapy, if only recently; so I stood up too: 'I won't speak to you unless you speak to me with fairness and respect.'

Fairness and respect . . . Fairness and respect . . . How many times did I repeat my pathetic request?

He stepped closer. He was shorter than me. He stabbed the air with his finger in my face: 'You have a problem with anger!'

'*I* do?'

'There are things you do not know!'

'About what?'

He repeated: 'There are things you do not know!'

'Then tell me.'

But he wouldn't. Or couldn't. He follwed me into the house. My mother swept down the stairs and clung to his side. 'We're just being frank!' she cried; she seemed delighted, almost titillated. I'd never seen them so in love before. And in that moment I knew who they were. What they were. I had always known but now they were unmasked.

Then, again, bellowing: 'There are things you do not know!'

Fairness . . . respect . . . my voice quavering, my fists and shoulders coiling; I could've knocked him flat, could've broken a chair or the table with his bulk.

Instead I saved myself. By containing myself. By choosing to be fairer, more respectful to him—than him—I might martyr myself, but there would be no refusing this gift. I exited trembling through the back door, and in my rental car driving home—to my home, to my future—I realized I would never see my parents again. It had happened, finally. It was all over. I was me.

*

To recap: crisis explodes, confounds, remakes who we are. The drama leads us through one crisis, then on toward another.

Every character, certainly our protagonist—who is me, who is you—is altered by the odyssey. The ho-hum hero's journey is, of course, an ancient, Aristotelean artifact, individualistic, which is to say capitalistic and paternalistic. Yet the marketplace in New York and London has demanded this sort of play for as long as the marketplace has existed.

But is the model accurate? Does it have to be? Is anything we think we know about the theatre—and writing plays for it—meaningful now that there is no theatre? Or more constructively: How can we re-forge the character of the American theatre in the crucible of our current crisis?

Speaking as a survivor, I have stood at this crossroads before. After cancer, after the astonishment of being told that I no longer possessed 'evidence of disease,' the last thing I wanted to do was 'get back to normal'—the mythical normal of 'how it was before.' My normal life had seemingly spawned my near-demise, and my wife's too, so I recoiled from regression of any kind. I wanted to repent and live differently. Some difference was easy: I renounced red meat, sugar and alcohol, ingesting daily supplements of turmeric, megadoses of Vitamin D and tree nuts by the handful. I felt purer, clarified by the trials of my treatment and confinement, and I wished to carry this wisdom with me into my new life.

Sometimes I wanted to never write again. I wondered what I had been doing it for in the first place, whether it had ever actually been a choice. I wanted to burn much of my old life to the ground and start over as somebody else, somebody new, having cast aside forever every superstition, every fairy tale I'd ever told myself about myself, now that I had finally learned the lesson of chaos. I was seeking a post-traumatic revolution.

What will the theatre look like after? Will the theatre still exist?—revivified? reborn? What are *your* ideas: Drive-in live theatre? Re-inhabited, half-ruinous amphitheaters? Theatre for lonesome drabs of intrepid spectators dispersed inside cavernous auditoriums (cheered by ferns)? Will the withering of our theatrical ecosystem allow for the sprouting of a grassroots, more demotic theatre, declaimed from the flatbeds of trucks in baseball fields and Walmart parking lots? Will COVID-19 become the subject and setting of every play, so that designers can costume actors in the latest PPE? Will audiences have to have their nasal cavities swabbed at will-call windows, provided that reliable rapid testing is ever achieved? When will the vaccines arrive? Will audiences feel comfortable taking their seats again? Will they trust? Will they even be the same audience they were before?

And will the theaters themselves change? Will only the wealthiest organizations and institutions emerge after the Great Pause, having hibernated off the fat of their endowments and bailouts and the patronage of the usual wealthy suspects? Will the protestations of our collapse succeed in forcing a restructuring or demolishing of the theatre's overwhelmingly white and male hierarchies? Will artistic directors and other well-compensated staff voluntarily (or otherwise) relinquish their fiefdoms every few years for the sake of new blood, if not for the sake of justice? Will playwrights finally receive a living wage for their mostly thankless labor?

Without a reconstituted Federal Theatre Project, will our dramatists turn their hands exclusively to other genres like TV and film, or to writing poetry (not likely), novels and journalism (see poetry), or to more 'essential' livelihoods like grocery cashiering, facemask stitching, nursing?

Nobody knows now. What a fearsome, exhilarating, depressing lacuna in our lives: inside the whirlwind of unknowing, the eye of the cyclone, the lull after the quake before the tsunami hits, where and when we may find ourselves prone to oracular utterances in the first-person plural. Such as:

When the disaster came—of my brother's leap, of my parents' disowning, of my wife's and my cancers, of this our too-novel coronavirus—it was accidental and inevitable. Some saw it coming. It was inappropriately comical. It was dreadful. None of it was necessarily survivable. When the plague came it was an act of God, it was 'nature healing,' it was wildfires racing downhill into hurricanes. It was the comet. We grew bored. We grew our beards; our roots were showing. We got fat, and skinny. Underemployed and uninsured, we felt always pressed for time. Our children befriended loneliness and cried at our windows looking out. Time was a slog requiring patience, cocktails, THC . . .

With the infected wind we dreamed of decamping in our rented Airstreams for the mountains; we DMed old friends to see were they still alive, and had they forgotten us and had we forgiven them (not yet). We conceived of as many projects as we abandoned. We came to terms with what we could not live without; while eating up our nest egg . . . We mail-ordered wedding rings. Our marital spats continued apace. We filed in our minds for divorce. We found ourselves pregnant again. We expected. We expired. We baked more bread.

When the cataclysm, when the calamity, when the catastrophe—we couldn't breathe. We said their names. We reckoned, demanded recompense. We took to the streets, Pentecostal, with our tongues of fire. We toppled the statues of historical characters we barely remembered because we could not forget. We were reminded that every story happens before it can be told. We were perplexed, to say the least.

When the deprivations and the degradations and the punishments and the police, when the jackboots and the flashbangs and the tear gas and the unmarked vans: we defied, prophesying in the summer sunlight and late at night into the faces of our bone-cold screens.

And when it is all over . . . after the war, after disease, after revolution and its medicines . . . we may find that we lost our minds, for a while. We forgot who we were. Who we are. We will have to find out. And the theatre as always will show us.

Acknowledgments

Earlier versions of these chapters first appeared in the following publications: 'Time and the Theatre' in *The Missouri Review* and excerpted by *Literary Hub* in 2018; 'Unspeakable: Speech on Stage' in the anthology *As We Were Saying: Sewanee Writers on Writing* (LSU Press, 2021); 'Surviving Conflict' in *The Paris Review* online in 2019 and delivered at the United States Air Force Academy in Colorado Springs, Colorado, as the 2019 David L. Jannetta Distinguished Lecture in War, Literature & the Arts; and 'Identity in Crisis' excerpted by *Literary Hub* in 2020. I am indebted to the following editors, friends, supporters, and instigators: Wyatt Prunty, Leah Stewart, Megan Roberts, Adam Latham, Gwen Kirby, Naomi Iizuka, Adam Ross, Lauren Yee, Liliana Padilla, Ken Weitzman, Speer Morgan, Evelyn Rogers, Christian Kiefer, Nadja Spiegelman, Emily Nemens, David Yezzi, J. M. Tyree, Donald Anderson, Jesse Goolsby, Jonny Diamond, Jonathan Reiber, Ann Barham, David Collard, Jacob Appel, the 2020 Orchard Project Professional's Lab (Aitor Basauri, Neena Beeber, Stephen Belber, Jaime Castañeda, Kristoffer Diaz, Ari Edelson, Zachary Fine, Jessica Hecht, James Kennedy, Krista Knight, Dionne McClain-Freeney, Toby Park, Jill Sobule, Yohann Trépanier), and my 2020 Sewanee Writers' Conference master class (Stacey Isom Campbell, Ron Gephart, Jacqueline Graham, Rachel Heng, Teresa Hudson, Vicki Meagher, Jonathon Mello, Helene Montagna, Lina Patel, Patrick Wohlmut). I wish to thank also my playwriting agent Beth Blickers, who has been with me—and for me—since the beginning. Lastly I offer my boundless gratitude to my wife Jessica St. Clair, always my first and most cherished reader.

CB *editions*

Founded in 2007, CB editions publishes chiefly short fiction and poetry, including work in translation. Poetry titles include three collections by Dan O'Brien. Books can be ordered from www.cbeditions.com.